1001 IDEAS FOR
STONEWORK
The Ultimate Sourcebook

1001 IDEAS FOR
STONEWORK
The Ultimate Sourcebook

RICHARD WILES

IDEAS & INSPIRATION FOR:
- Stone Floors & Countertops
- Natural Stone Walls & Fireplaces
- Landscape Features

Creative Publishing
international

First published in North America in 2009 by
Creative Publishing international
400 First Avenue North
Suite 300
Minneapolis, MN 55401
800 328 3895
www.creativepub.com

**Creative Publishing
international**

A Marshall Edition
Conceived, edited, and designed by
Marshall Editions
The Old Brewery
6 Blundell Street
London N7 9BH
U.K.
www.marshalleditions.com

For Marshall Editions:
Publisher: Jenni Johns
Art Director: Ivo Marloh
Managing Editor: Paul Docherty
Project Editors: Amy Head and Jenny Doubt
New Title Development Manager: Deborah Hercun
Design: 3rd-i
Indexer: Lisa Footitt
Production: Nikki Ingram

For Creative Publishing international:
President/CEO: Ken Fund
VP for Sales & Marketing: Kevin Hamric
Publisher: Bryan Trandem
Managing Editor: Tracy Stanley
Editor: Jennifer Gehlhar
Production Managers: Linda Halls, Laura Hokkanen
Creative Director: Michele Lanci-Altomare
Senior Design Managers: Jon Simpson, Brad Springer
Design Manager: James Kegley

ISBN-10: 1-58923-459-6
ISBN-13: 978-1-58923-459-8

A catalog record for this book is available from the
Library of Congress

Current printing (last digit)
10 9 8 7 6 5 4 3 2 1

Originated in Hong Kong by Modern Age
Printed and bound in China

Front cover image: M. Angelo/Corbis
Back cover image: ChantalS/Fotolia

Contents

Introduction

Despite the perception of natural stone as hard, cold, and dense, in reality it is a surprisingly subtle material that is ideal for decorating the interior of your home. Natural stone is incredibly durable, moisture- and grease-resistant, hygienic, and stylish. Outside, tough stone slabs and smaller pavers make an immensely strong surface for driveways, patios, and paths, while stone walls give gardens both structure and form. Stone statues, urns, and other ornaments add a distinctive decorative touch to any design.

One of the essential materials used to create tools, buildings, and other structures for thousands of years, stone is as relevant today as it was in prehistoric times. Stone is an eminently versatile and beautiful material that is available in many forms due to the aid of modern manufacturing methods. Reconstituted stone can also be cast in molds to reproduce classic profiles, statues, and other ornamentation.

Thousands of years ago, quarried stone was employed to construct houses, barns, and other buildings. Initially, irregular shaped rocks were bonded with mud or cement or simply laid dry. The Romans were masters at constructing buildings and bridges from interlocking stone without the need for a bonding agent such as cement. Rough stonework was typically rendered with mortar or else left bare, perhaps whitewashed. Later, stone was cut into large, square-shaped "ashlar" blocks and it continued to be used to build, or face, the walls of houses, farm and industrial buildings, and apartments well into the 20th century.

Where such stonework survives, it deserves to be shown off to its best advantage rather than concealed—as often happened in misguided attempts at being "modern"—behind uniform coats of plaster or drywall. Stonework should not be considered an outmoded

material best reserved for country cottages; it can be used just as effectively in modern interiors, where it can lend texture and color to an otherwise stark design. Today's treated stonework is often not the pitted, rugged material of yesteryear, but a sleek, shiny, stylish, hard surface with fantastic aesthetic qualities.

Where no original stonework exists it can easily be installed. Stone doesn't have to be supplied as cumbersome blocks. There are many relatively lightweight, slim stone tiles that can be applied to an existing wall.

Larger, thicker stone slabs and tiles make an unsurpassable flooring material, particularly in areas that receive heavy traffic such as entrances and hallways and areas that are subject to moisture such as kitchens and bathrooms. There are many types of stone that are naturally impervious to grease and spills.

Stone has a bad reputation for feeling cold—helpful for cooling a room in a hot country, but uncomfortable in colder climates. However, modern underfloor heating systems minimize this drawback. These systems generate radiant heat that warms not only the floor but the entire room. When combined with underfloor heating, stone is an excellent choice for a living room.

Opposite: An imposing portico faced with dry-stone walling provides a visual link between this colonial-style house and its rural setting.

Below: A weathered, ribbed stone urn spilling with scented plants adds texture and form amidst the foliage of this planting bed.

Living Rooms

Living rooms should be designed primarily for comfort, providing a space where you and the family can relax alone or entertain guests. If you have young children, the inevitable falls of a toddler might mean that hard stone is not the best choice of flooring. Used on both the walls and floor, stone dictates the character of the room. Confine it to a single feature wall or fireplace to avoid a dominant "enclosing" effect. A light-colored floor—mellow sandstone, pastel limestone, or milky marble with delicate veins—makes a room appear larger and suits modern furniture and light accessories rather than dark wood. Sheer drapes and pastel upholstery help create a bright, fresh environment. Dark flooring such as slate or basalt visually decreases the height of a room—an advantage if the ceilings are tall. Riven-faced sandstone slabs are most at home in a period, country-style setting.

①

②

③

⑤

④

① The lofty stone wall of this barn conversion is complemented by a roughly plastered dividing wall. The height of the room is minimized by an oak staircase and ceiling beams. Rectangular sandstone flooring provides a neutral base for a suite in oatmeal upholstery.

② Purity is achieved in this striking minimalist interior. White walls are reflected in the cloudy sheen of limestone floor slabs, and the overall effect is softened by a long-pile rug.

③ This open-plan living room and kitchen is floored with beige sandstone slabs and an area of toning woodstrip. The otherwise wasted space beneath the stone-look concrete staircase is filled with large, rounded boulders as a novel decorative touch.

④ Combining natural elements of reclaimed light pine and durable, long-lasting slate makes this green-friendly living environment both warm and efficient. Slate stone is strong and can easily withstand extreme heat emanating from the fireplace. This stone can be safely used for years with no fear of breakage.

⑤ An intricate but neutral geometric mosaic of tumbled travertine complements the base of the pillar it surrounds, itself adorned with contrasting mosaic fragments.

Dining Rooms and Conservatories

Dining rooms are made for entertaining, and you have the option to create a cozy, intimate atmosphere or a bright, airy feel. Adding stone to a dining room can effectively create a focal point. For example, a panel of stone tiles on the lower part of wooden wainscoted walls acts as a visual reference. However, you should avoid integrating too many elements in a design. When strong features clash, the resulting environment is not suited to relaxed, after-dinner conversation.

Conservatories should, without exception, be bright and airy; and lustrous marble floor tiles excel in this respect. Create a feature of the floor—perhaps with octagonal tiles and darker-colored diamond infills—and keep the furnishing minimal. When selecting furniture take into account that metal chairs create marks when scraped across a stone floor, and even some shoes will scar softer stone. It may be wise, in these cases, to invest in a rug to place beneath the table and chairs.

①

③

②

④

① This airy, sunlit interior is achieved by offsetting mottled limestone slabs, which exude a pastel glow, with pure white walls. The painted panel above the walnut dining table mirrors this effect.

② A bold, decorative statement for an otherwise cool, understated interior, this imposing stone urn shows how to achieve a successful eclectic mix with little effort.

③ An elegant dining room with a novel twist: pale rustic stonework is selectively exposed beneath the smooth plaster of a deep maroon wall.

④ The granite walls of this farmhouse, patched with hollow clay bricks, contrast beautifully with polished wood cabinets and a dainty dining set.

⑤ Octagonal Victorian-style floor tiles in beige limestone contrast with diamond shapes in dark gray, which pick out the shade of the iron furniture.

⑥ Slate is anything but the plain gray you might imagine. In this conservatory, metallic tones and swirling infusions suggest the great outdoors that lie just beyond.

⑤

⑥

Kitchens

Hygiene, ease of cleaning, and resistance to stains, spills, and water are priorities in the kitchen, and stonework offers all of these qualities. However, many types of stonework, particularly for floors, do need sealing to preserve their appearance and durability. Choose floor tiles or slabs with a nonslip surface, and avoid small-scale units and recessed joints, where dirt can collect. One drawback with using such a hard surface is that stone can be tiring to stand on for long periods. Also, kitchenware and other breakables may shatter if dropped.

On walls, stone tiles can be used for a backsplash behind the sink or an easy-clean surface between a countertop and the underside of wall cabinets. As an alternative to the conventional combination of stainless steel or porcelain sink and wooden countertop, choose from the beautiful sink basins and countertops made of granite, marble, Jerusalem stone, or slate. The color range is vast, and stone countertops are able to withstand hot pans and resist scratches.

① Black granite kitchen countertops, polished to an ultrasmooth mirror finish, are a modern option that combines hygiene, practicality, and lustrous good looks.

② Unlikely bedfellows, a stainless steel kitchen unit harmonizes well here with the random, multicolored stonework on the wall. An original stone sink has also been put to use.

③ The traditional flooring of English farmhouses, Yorkstone—here in a complex geometric pattern—complements rustic kitchens. Common features of this style include pine cupboards, wicker baskets, and country-style accessories.

④ Mottled, gray-brown travertine flooring gives this period-style kitchen an air of austerity, especially when matched with cream cabinets for a well-blended color scheme.

⑤ The deep orange wood of this kitchen would have been monotonous without the visual relief of oyster-colored slate flooring. The tones reflect the metallic finish of the refrigerator and blend with the stainless steel cabinet hardware, accessories, and baseboards.

①

②

④

⑤

①

Bathrooms, Wet Rooms, and Shower Rooms

Resistance to water is a flooring prerequisite for bathrooms, wet rooms, and showers. This makes large stone tiles the best choice: the fewer joints there are, the less likelihood there is of moisture seeping through. For sheer opulence, there's little that beats lustrous, veined marble for bathroom floors and walls. You can also buy tubs, sinks, and toilets made of marble (and other stone). Complete the classical look with decorative stone columns and Roman-style mosaic pictures on the walls or floor. Alternatively, for a sense of drama, consider using the tarnished metal look of slate tiles for a wall-to-wall, floor-to-ceiling wet room, or go for the muted look with delicate pastel sandstone, chrome fittings, and a glass shower enclosure. Bear in mind that stone with a smooth, shiny surface will be dangerously slippery when wet.

① Lustrous green and white veined marble tiles, used on the floor, walls, and bath surround, create an air of opulence accentuated by the reflective surfaces of the glass shower enclosure and mirror.

② Copper-colored slate on the walls and floor creates a tarnished metal effect that contributes to the minimalist tone of this bathroom, where surfaces and fittings have a linear quality.

③ Stone is ideal for use in the bathroom, as is evident here: reflective black marble walls contrast with gray-veined white marble flooring, black and white mosaics are used in the shower, and even the bowl and vanity shelf are hewn from white marble.

④ On the walls of this bathroom, subway tiles in beige are accentuated by white grout lines to create a grid from which grained-wood fittings and slimline fixtures appear to hang.

⑤ Random-shaped slabs of gray granite clad the walls of this shower enclosure. The color of unpolished brass fittings mimics the streaks in the stonework, adding detail to the overall effect.

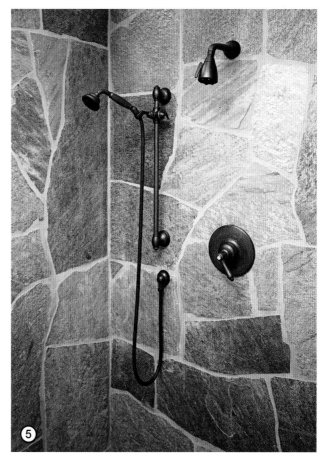

Hallways, Staircases, and Bedrooms

Usually extending from the front entrance of the house, hallways receive heavy traffic and constant exposure to dirt. A flooring that can be easily brushed clean and washed to remove marks is vital. Stone tiles make an excellent, hardwearing surface that is scratch resistant. Choose light colors for a small hallway, and consider using a rug to soften stone flooring in a large hallway. Complement the flooring in the rooms adjoining the hallway, or even continue the same material into other rooms.

① Cool, pale travertine is stylish in minimal settings like this and doesn't overwhelm the space as dark stone might.

② A modern take on a classical style, this winding staircase is made of common building materials but the treads and risers are faced.

③ Light is reflected into a spacious hallway by the luscious gloss of marble. Subtle color is added in the veins, flecks, and mottling of the stone.

Stone flooring and stone wall treatments may not be obvious choices for bedrooms, where most people prefer a cozy atmosphere. However, floor tiling in muted tones or even dark slate both work well, particularly if you use rugs to soften the effect. Exposed stone walls painted white, cream, or pale blue—or tiles that resemble natural stone walls—can create a Mediterranean feel.

④ An eccentric, homemade fire surround of jumbled boulders is coupled with a log mantel to create an unconventional centerpiece in a rustic-themed bedroom.

⑤ Polished limestone slabs and white walls create a cool atmosphere in a hot climate. Dark wood furniture contrasts with the otherwise all-cream room to help add definition and visual interest.

Patios, Paths, and Steps

An area of stone slabs adjoining the house becomes an outdoor extension to your home, where you can relax or dine during the summer (and, with the use of patio heaters, during mild winters). Break up a large area of slabs with smaller-scale stone setts or cobbles, defining a geometric shape within the paving. Incorporate planters within a large patio and define the area with stone walls topped with slabs, which can double as seats. Use stone steps as a route from the patio to lower or higher levels of the yard. Paths of slabs, flagstones, or loose gravel can provide access to other areas. Remember that paths don't need to be straight but can take a circuitous route to increase the feeling of space. When planning, ensure that paths and steps are wide enough to accommodate your guests and your activities.

⑤

① The clean lines of this Asian-inspired garden incorporate platforms of white stone, creating a floating effect above the bamboo-fenced pond.

② A simple line of stepping stones winding its way across a lawn is one of the easiest types of garden paths to make.

③ The materials used in building and landscaping this forest dwelling are harmonious with its surroundings. The steps, walls, and patio have been formed with local stone.

④ This idiosyncratic house, sided with weathered diagonal planks, is accessed by steps that have been hewn from an outcrop of rock. The harshness is softened by plantings.

⑤ To create a patio with a unique decorative pattern such as this, draw a floral or geometric design on squared paper and then use an angle grinder to cut colored sandstone slabs to shape.

⑥ Straight-edged slabs can be used to create a curving path with precise cuts.

⑦ Large sandstone slabs in pink, yellow, blue, and buff form a grand frontage and patio here. This area also makes effective use of balustrading for definition.

⑥

⑦

Landscaping Features

Stone walls form the skeleton of a garden, defining planting areas and natural changes in the landscape. Dry-stone walls, in which the stones are simply laid without mortar, are suited to informal or country style gardens, while coursed stonework—stone blocks bonded with mortar—is in keeping with more formal designs. Create a waterfall with natural boulders forming a bank and a watercourse that can be pumped and recirculated. In rock gardens, large stones might appear to break through the earth in natural outcrops; plantings of heather, alpines, and other plants from rocky regions can add to the natural appearance. You can also use large boulders decoratively, positioned artfully on the surface to create an area of interest in a lawn or as a backdrop to a planting bed. Consider using cobblestones or loose gravel combed with interesting geometric lines to create a garden with Japanese styling, or simply use stones to define the edge of a path of gravel or slabs.

① Landscaping can embrace all aspects of your yard. Dot granite slabs around a lawn for a path that doubles as a rock garden.

② The boundary walls of this Mediterranean villa are made less imposing by virtue of having been constructed from random sizes and shapes of mellow sandstone.

③ Large rocks and outcrops can be used predominantly for decorative effect, as is shown here. The intriguing shapes of the rocks provides a source of constant fascination.

④ Arranging stones haphazardly on sloping or stepped ground will create a natural waterfall. Use a large urn as an original and quirky source of water.

Outdoor Structures

Use stonework to build gazebos, pergolas, seating areas defined by walls, or raised patios from which you can admire the garden or watch the sun go down. Create built-in stone tables, benches, and other furniture from natural or cast stone.

Prefabricated gazebos are available in classical or Gothic style. These elegant roofed structures may contain a statue as a decorative statement or a seat for taking a quiet moment. Pergolas are arched structures, generally erected along the length of a path or walkway or running along a wall, which incorporate a trellis roof or framework of rafters over which climbing plants are grown. Build the supporting pillars from coursed stonework, or use prefabricated Romanesque columns made from reconstituted stone to hold the trellis. Place a stone urn or statue at the end of the pergola as a focal point.

①

②

① Create a romantic area for dining in a quiet corner of the garden, with an elegant brick-walled raised pool adorned with stone columns. Illuminate the columns with subtle spotlights and furnish with Mediterranean-style furniture.

② An open-air living room such as this can be created with a stone-built exterior fireplace, stone columns (to define the perimeter of the space), and a ceiling of stout wooden rafters.

③ A simple prefabricated stone firepit, fueled by natural gas, provides warmth for chilly evenings on the patio. Add a suspended cauldron and cook al fresco.

④ Terra-cotta tiles form a distinct border around this raised stone patio. Speckled gray tiles cover the seating area as well as the sides and stairs.

⑤ This black granite planter, with smooth granite coping, separates the flow of a streamlike pathway and doubles as an informal sitting area.

Statues and Garden Ornaments

Add an air of mystery and intrigue to your garden by positioning a statue half-concealed by shrubs or trees, as the centerpiece of a lawn, or as the focal point at the end of a walkway or pergola.

You'll find stone figures of animals such as lions, birds, and horses to adorn your yard, as well as mythical and fantastic creatures. Obelisks, stone globes, sundials, and other stone effigies can also be used to good effect in creating style. It is possible to obtain original, carved stone sculptures, but modern reproductions in cast limestone, produced from original molds, weather just like real stone and are much more affordable. Birdbaths not only add a focal point but will also entice feathered visitors. Fountains come in a range of prefabricated parts and in numerous sizes—linked to a pump and water supply, they will add visual fascination and the delightful sound of babbling water to the yard.

① A gargoyle will bring a sense of otherworldly mischief to your garden. This hunched character has been molded from a pale-toned cast limestone.

② Add a touch of the Orient to your garden with a distinctive ornament such as this Japanese stone lantern, the perfect complement to plants such as the azalea shown. The lantern is also a practical touch, shedding light at night.

③ Use a large stone ornament, such as this well-worn antique urn, as the centerpiece to a patio. Here, small-scale setts reflect the texture of the urn, while larger slabs arranged in a circular pattern complement its rounded shape.

④ Cherubs are perennial darlings of decoration, both indoors and outdoors. For classical charm, a mossy fountain like this one would be difficult to top.

⑤ This original sculpted fountain looks great amongst shrubs but would also hold its own in a more prominent position.

⑥ The timeless grandeur of a classical statue, perhaps placed at the end of a path or in a quiet corner of the garden, suggests an air of calm, inviting guests to linger and savor the atmosphere of the garden.

①

②

③

⑤

④

⑥

House Exteriors

Stonework can transform the appearance of a house, but it must be carried out sensitively if you want to avoid an eyesore—and the wrath of the neighbors and planning authorities! A flat façade of rendered or plain brick can be clad with stone tiles applied with a mortar-based adhesive. You might opt for the traditional coursed stonework look or a random effect of irregular-shaped stones.

A more traditional option—often employed on woodframe buildings—is to clad the walls, or just a feature wall, with slate tiles. These can even prevent rain from entering. The installation process is the same as that for hanging wood shingles or covering a pitched roof. Stonework porches are available as kits for professional installation, and other stonework embellishments such as porticos can add a grand touch.

① A flight of steps constructed with coarse dry-stone risers and smooth, gray treads is matched in tone by the tiles hung on the walls. The wall tile is a good DIY project and a fairly inexpensive update that drastically improves curb appeal.

② Natural stone cladding with rough, riven faces invest this modern house with a touch of rural charm, softening the angularity of the raised terrace.

③ Stone cladding in buff and sand tones, with accents of orange, faces this modern property. Elegant, molded window surrounds add contrast in tone and texture.

④ Combine modern lines with a rough stone texture for stylish cladding that will still blend with natural elements. The grasses and flower pots at this entranceway soften the overall effect.

①

Interior Walls and Floors

Faced with the blank canvas of a room—for example, plain walls and a wooden or concrete floor—you need the inspiration to decide on a theme or a character for the space. Your first task is to determine how you want to use the room. This will help you decide which features are essential and which you would like to include. If you have existing furniture that you want to keep, you're halfway to establishing your scheme. Now think outside the box: what benefits could you gain from using stone?

Floorboards look fantastic when sealed and varnished, and they come in a variety of exotic wood types. However, they're prone to damage from furniture, scratch easily, can be draughty, and can leave splinters in the feet! Carpet is undeniably warm underfoot and insulating but is also prone to staining, wears out relatively quickly, and requires tiresome vacuuming. Stone tiles and slabs are incredibly durable, long lasting, and can be washed down to remove marks; a quick flick with a brush will return them to spick-and-span condition.

The base on which you lay stone tiles must be perfectly flat, sound, and free from grease and moisture. The best surface is properly leveled and smoothed concrete. While is it possible to lay slabs directly onto an existing solid concrete floor, this may not produce the best results. Wood floors are subject to movement under loading, temperature, and humidity. However, it is possible to lay stone slabs over a surface of tongue-and-groove boards, particleboard, or plywood, provided that it is completely rigid and stable to prevent the tiles from breaking or debonding.

When it comes to walls, wallpaper and other wallcoverings can be luxurious, but many types—particularly the common printed rolls—pass in and out of fashion with increasing regularity. A plain, painted surface is the easiest yet most unimaginative option. Stone wall tiles, on the other hand, infuse any room with a distinctive and unique character—no one tile is identical to another.

Real stone tiles are moisture- and grease-resistant, attractive, and long lasting. Although all stone is tough, some types possess more resistance to abrasion and acids. Wall tiles in living areas are not susceptible to such damage, but kitchen backsplashes should be made of stone that copes with cooking splashes and abrasion from cleaning agents; bathroom tiling should not only be highly resistant to water but also to soaps and detergents.

Most people think "gray and monotonous" when they think of stone, but that is far from the truth! There's a vast range of shades available in stone, ranging from white through yellows, sand tones, browns, and pinks to reds, blues, and greens, right up to black—in fact, the whole spectrum is represented. Often, individual stones incorporate trace elements of other minerals, strictly speaking "defects," which nevertheless create fascinating patterns, glistening fragments, and delicate veins.

Furthermore, stonework is versatile enough to be incorporated into a setting that also includes other materials, blending in well with floorboards, carpet, and wall coverings, and furniture both old and new. Stone is the ultimate chameleon in decorative terms.

Opposite: Earthy tones are used in a sumptuous blend of textures in this living room. A patchwork of rugged stone on the walls is complemented by polished floor slabs in terra-cotta sandstone and an imposing ceiling in a rich treacle lacquer.

Below: Black slate lines the walls and floor in this striking bathroom, where the pure lines of a white porcelain sink and modern chrome faucet add contrast.

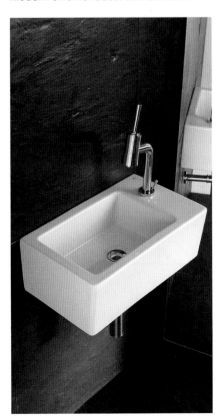

Exposed Stone

In many older homes, rough stonework is coated with plaster or, worse still, tough cement veneer in an attempt to "modernize" and help reduce the dust that tends to afflict old stone. Alternatively, stone walls might be concealed beneath drywall boards fixed to wood battens. Fortunately, in most cases, you'll be able to remove the cladding and give the stonework the exposure it deserves.

If you're lucky enough to live in a stone house, barn, mill, or warehouse conversion with exposed walls, you already have the basis to create a stunning interior with little effort. You may need to renovate defective mortar joints. Many older buildings were built with nothing more than mud between the stones. These stones and grout lines should be sealed.

① The enormous stone blocks used to construct this barn conversion have been exposed and their distinctive shape, texture, and tone are now used as the theme of this sunny room.

② The complex texture and tone of this exposed stone wall marries well with the smooth, black-stained wood floor and yellow vanity unit with its unfussy white basin.

③ This exposed sandstone wall appears as an extension of the view glimpsed through the floor-to-ceiling window. Naturally occurring colors are echoed in the lacquered green vanity unit, earthy rug, and cool, honed stone floor.

④ Sun-drenched colors and textures infuse this bright, airy room with the vibrant flavors of the Mediterranean.

⑤ There's nothing subtle about this bold feature of exposed stone, which necessitates similar strength of character in the choice of furniture.

⑥ A touch of Greece: the walls of this bedroom are painted pure white in the ubiquitous "asvesti," a perfect partner to Mediterranean blue. If authentic, blue-tinged whitewash is unavailable, use non-lime-based alternatives.

⑦ Exposed stonework is taken to the extreme in this unique bathroom, where toughened glass "gabions" filled in with white beach stones form the walls.

Exposed stone is like hidden treasure that has been uncovered. The colors and shapes of the stones and the bonds used to construct the walls are frequently complex and yield a wealth of fantastic patterns. Your role is to determine how best to enhance the character of the stonework. This may involve nothing more than accentuating the shapes of the stones with colored mortar or profiled pointing (beveled or recessed below the face of the stones). If the stonework proves to be less attractive in its exposed state, give the entire wall a coat of whitewash or one of the modern stone paints, which come in a fabulous array of pastel tones.

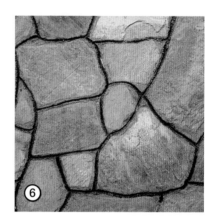

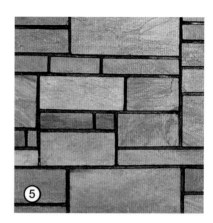

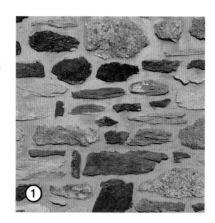

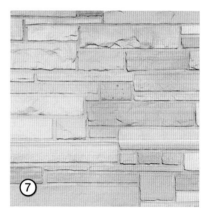

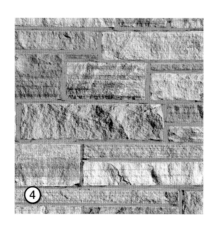

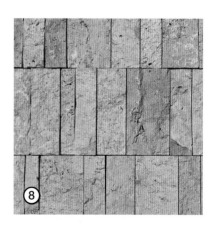

① Partially exposed granite
② Unpolished granite in random shapes
③ Rough basalt
④ Sandstone in pink shades
⑤ Coursed Greek "plaka" slate
⑥ Random Greek "plaka" slate
⑦ Sandstone in orange shades
⑧ Unsealed granite in a vertical bond
⑨ Pink travertine with colored pointing
⑩ Sealed sandstone
⑪ Chiseled Jerusalem stone
⑫ Blue and pink slate
⑬ Golden sandstone
⑭ Multilayered stone with cement
   mortar slurry
⑮ Sandstone with lime mortar
⑯ Cotswold limestone
⑰ River-stone chips
⑱ Antiqued stained granite
⑲ Gray, orange, and yellow sandstone
⑳ Varnished slate

Stone Tiles

Stone wall tiles can be used to decorate—and even to help insulate—the interior walls of your home. The riven or weather-beaten faces of split or naturally worn stone introduce sensuous textures to a decorative scheme, while stone's lustrous sheen and earthy colors combine to create an atmosphere of enveloping warmth.

Unlike other mass-produced hard tiles, each stone tile is unique in its textures and surface patterning. Marble, for example, is typically infused with elaborate veining and mottling; sandstone can be finely streaked; basalt is pitted with thousands of tiny pinpricks; and slate has a flaky, laminated look. Coloring will even vary subtly within batches. Each installation, therefore, is invested with its own character.

If used wall-to-wall or floor-to-ceiling— perhaps in conjunction with stone or other hard flooring—stone can be too dominant, making a room appear dark and small. It's wise, therefore, to reserve stone for feature areas: fireplaces, backsplashes, and isolated wall sections.

①

②

③

④

① Use stone tile sheets against one section of a wall to add texture without overwhelming other elements in a room. Limestone and sandstone have been combined here.

② Old and new looks combine with ease in this sophisticated kitchen, where the deep brown, matte slate lines of the wall resonate behind the chocolate brown stove.

③ The prominence of white marble streaked with gray veining adds to the effect of space in this shower room.

④ These mottled sandstone slabs, with a gently undulating surface texture, are installed in a staggered bond, which is accentuated by bold white grout lines.

Stone flooring is highly attractive and immensely strong, and in time it will assume the pleasant patina of age. Many of the stone tiles used on walls can also be used on floors, though in some cases those intended for floors are larger and thicker due to the extra traffic and loading they will be subjected to. When choosing flooring, it's best to opt for the tiles that have a smooth (but still nonslip) finish, rather than those with deeply riven or pitted faces, in which dirt will soon collect.

The range of colors, patterns, and textures of stone floor tiles and slabs is huge, and will complement all styles of décor, whether rustic, traditional, or modern. Of the numerous types of stone available, granite is one of the most popular because of its hardness—second only to diamond—and its consequent durability.

Limestone, Jerusalem stone, and sandstone are favorite alternatives because of their subtle coloration and rustic quality. Marble and travertine, with their mottled, creamy colors, veining, and lustrous sheen, are best suited to formal settings.

Where you would like to make a bold, dramatic statement, slate and quartzite are hard to beat, with a distinctive color range that varies from gunmetal gray through rusty, metallic tones to pure black. Basalt is another dominant stone type with a presence that is hard to ignore.

① These riven Yorkstone slabs—the archetypal choice for a farmhouse kitchen floor—create a timeless, aged effect even when matched with modern fittings.

② Black riven slate floor slabs make durable flooring in this busy hallway. The subtle sheen of the slate reflects light from the glazed door, toning with the off-white staircase.

③ Retro-style furniture is shown off to best effect on this floor of cream limestone tiles. The soft mottling blends with the earthy feature wall and accessories.

④ Stone does not have to create a uniform look. Granite tiles, both square and rectangular and in a range of shades, provide the most ornate feature of this bathroom. A floor inset with a mosaic border finishes the job.

①

Types, Sizes, and Finishes

The size of a tile or slab is an important consideration: small units create a busier surface than larger, slab-sized panels. Reserve the smallest tiles for smaller areas of wall, or use them as borders to divide up a broader area of bigger tiles. Use large slabs for floors, breaking them up occasionally with a grid of rectangular tiles or diamond-shaped tiles fitted in the spaces between octagonal tiles. Stone wall tiles range in size from about 4 inches (10 cm) square to 4 x 8 inches (10 x 20 cm) and 12 x 8 inches (30 x 20 cm) and are usually about $\frac{3}{8}$ inch (1 cm) thick. Floor tiles vary in thickness from about $\frac{3}{8}$ inch to 2 inches (5 cm) and from approximately 15 x 15 inches (40 x 40 cm) and 23 x 15 inches (60 x 40 cm) to 31 x 15 inches (80 x 40 cm). Most suppliers offer other sizes for larger orders.

Tiles are fixed with cement-based adhesive and the joints between them are grouted. They can be butted up directly next to each other, spaced up to $\frac{1}{2}$ inch (1.5 cm) apart and recessed to accentuate the shape of the tiles, or set flush for a uniform effect. Tiles and slabs come with various finishes. A honed finish is smooth, flat matte, or low-sheen. Tumbled stone has undergone a blasting process to create a worn effect with rounded edges and subtle tone. A polished surface has a high-gloss sheen with enhanced coloring.

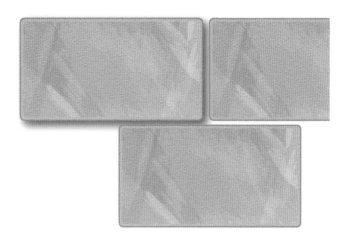

Rectangular tiles

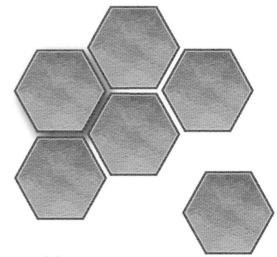

Octagonal tiles

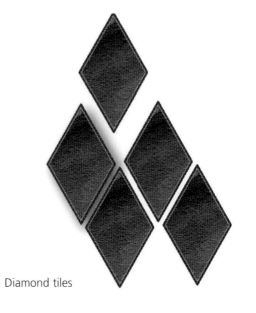

Diamond tiles

Long rectangular tiles ("subway tiles")

Thin rectangular tiles

Rectangular mosaic tiles

Square mosaic tiles

Square tiles

Tumbled stone is processed for a rustic, time-worn appearance. The stones are placed in a container along with an abrasive material—often silicon carbide grit—and lubricated with water. The container is then slowly rotated, causing the stones inside to tumble until they are smoothed and polished by the abrasive material. Tumbling also gives stone a nonslip surface. Numerous effects can be created by different degrees of tumbling. Basic tumbling will gently round off the edges of tiles and give the faces an antique look; more intense treatment produces a matte finish; further treatment will result in a highly polished appearance and irregular sizes.

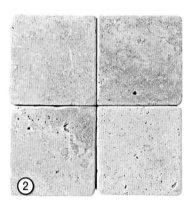

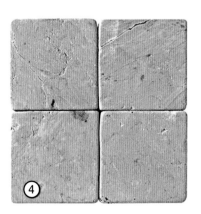

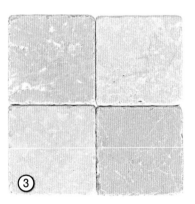

① Tumbled multicolored sandstone
② Tumbled white travertine
③ Tumbled white limestone
④ Tumbled gold sandstone
⑤ Tumbled copper granite
⑥ Tumbled cream sandstone
⑦ Tumbled brown marble
⑧ Tumbled light brown marble
⑨ Tumbled gray-green granite
⑩ Tumbled ivory travertine
⑪ Tumbled coral travertine
⑫ Tumbled, streaked pink sandstone
⑬ Tumbled beige limestone
⑭ Tumbled sienna travertine
⑮ Tumbled gray slate
⑯ Tumbled green slate

Travertine

Travertine—a dense form of calcium carbonate—is formed as a deposit left by calcite-rich water seeping though rocks. Its marblelike qualities have long been prized by sculptors, though it is more technically a type of limestone. Mined in countries such as Turkey, Mexico, Italy, and Peru, its surface is typically pitted with tiny voids caused by gases present when the rock was in its molten state. The tiling is shown to its best advantage when subtly lit, creating a delicate, warming glow and highlighting the attractive tones. Ideal for kitchen, bathroom, shower, or wet room walls, the faces of the tiles should—despite the impervious nature of the stone—be sealed against staining and moisture. Honed tiles have a contemporary appearance that is ideal when complemented by modern furniture, while rough-edged versions are more at home in a rustic setting.

① Mottled travertine tiles with white, pink, and rose blemishes create the three-dimensional appearance of a luminous nebula.

② Travertine with pronounced vertical streaks creates a wood-graining effect in this russet-toned bathroom.

③ A zigzag frieze created with clay penne shapes adds texture and toning color to an area of smoky travertine wall tiles with slim joint lines.

④ This sumptuous and stylish bathroom employs two shades of honed travertine, a delicate pink and a lustrous, tortoiseshell brown, to create a clean but warm glow.

⑤ Small versions of the same orange travertine tiles that appear on the walls of this Asian-inspired bathroom have been used on the floor.

①

②

③

⑤

④

Travertine floors blend perfectly with natural fabrics and materials to give a classic or contemporary look. Although travertine is durable, its honeycomb structure and visible surface pitting make it vulnerable to moisture and dirt. The cavities need to be filled, particularly when the stone is used on floors. Special stone resins are normally used on "filled" travertine to create a smoother finish. It is possible that in time some of the filler will become dislodged with the natural wearing of the floor. If this happens, there is no alternative than to refill the holes with a suitable resin or grout.

① Travertine varies in color, and this feature can be used to good effect; athough, it is important to avoid a concentration of similar shades in one area.

② Mixing and matching three different shapes of slabs or more creates interesting patterns in a floor.

③ Polished travertine has a subtle sheen, which provides a nonslip finish for wet areas such as the bathroom.

④ Lustrous, metallic-toned, polished travertine, used on the floor and walls of this bathroom, is partnered by brushed metal fittings and accessories to create a uniform style. The glass shower door casts attractive reflections.

Travertine is characteristically pale in color, from off-white to dark cream, including buff tones. Within each tile there are subtle surface variegations of random light and dark patches, so prior to final positioning on the wall or floor, it's best to dry lay them on the floor to avoid a concentration of similar shades. Tiles either come with their surfaces honed to a soft sheen, the tiny voids filled with a tough epoxy resin; unfilled, with more undulating and pitted faces for a coarser, more natural texture; or unfilled with a fine, brushed finish. Edges may be cut straight or left irregular with a wrinkled, "pillow" finish. Color intensifiers can also be used to enhance the base color of pale tones.

① Unfilled gold
② Unfilled muscat
③ Filled and honed honey
④ Unfilled salt and pepper
⑤ Unfilled red sunset
⑥ Unfilled light walnut
⑦ Antique-brushed, unfilled sea gray
⑧ Filled and polished, vein-cut light walnut
⑨ Filled, honed olive with streaks
⑩ Honed cloudy cream
⑪ Unfilled, tumbled coral
⑫ Unfilled dark walnut
⑬ Unfilled orange
⑭ Filled, honed tortoiseshell
⑮ Filled, honed cinnamon
⑯ Filled light pink
⑰ Unfilled, honed red
⑱ Filled, polished yellow with rose streaks
⑲ Unfilled white ivory
⑳ Filled, honed yellow

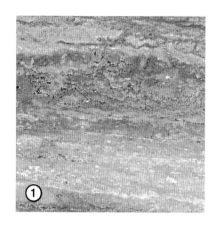

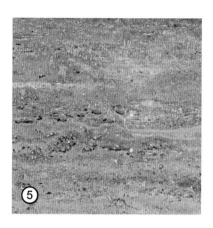

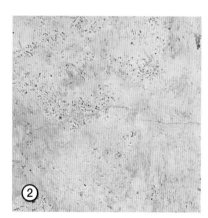

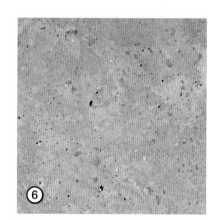

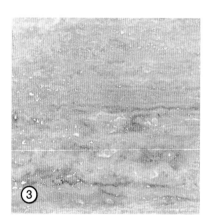

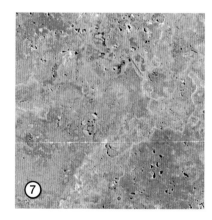

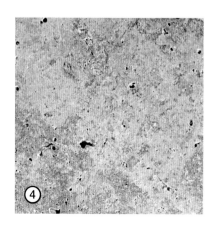

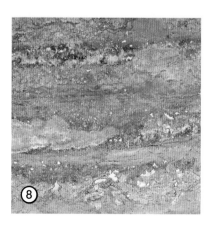

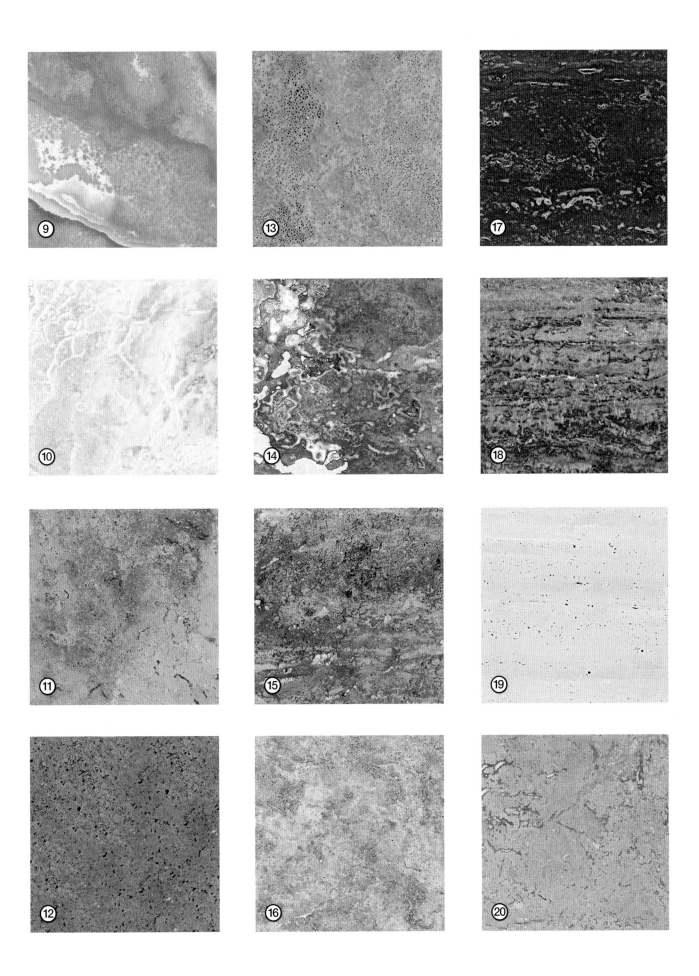

①

②

Marble

Marble is a very dense type of crystallized limestone formed over millions of years by heat and pressure within the earth's crust. This process results in a vast spectrum of colors, with characteristic mineral veining that contrasts with the base color. The density of this stone type allows it to be polished to a mirrorlike finish, though honed and tumbled varieties are also commonly used.

Marble is the classic stone—usually named after the area in which it was mined. It is found in many parts of Europe, Asia, India, and the U.S.A., but the best type is widely accepted as coming from Italy. Marble boasts an opulent look that has been used in palaces and grand buildings throughout history. As a cool stone, it is particularly successful if used on the walls of steamy bathrooms, shower rooms, and wet rooms, while less successful in living rooms and bedrooms (which, perhaps, require a more intimate treatment). Typical uses for marble wall tiles include forming a backsplash behind a basin or bath or a panel behind a toilet or bidet. While small tiles can add texture and shape to a plain wall, the most dramatic effects can be created with large sheets of marble, which show the veining patterns to their best effect without interruption.

① A panel of eggshell-colored marble is streaked with clouds of smoky blue-gray, adding texture in an otherwise glossy minimalist bathroom.

② The combination of an iridescent sheen with swirling, intense tones create an almost liquid appearance in this shell-like marble wall.

③

⑤

④

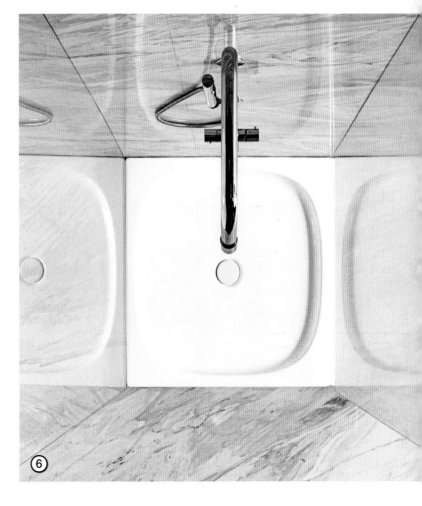

⑥

③ The milky marble bathroom walls and floor here provide an elegant backdrop to a delicate antique vanity unit.

④ Misty marble with gray veining is contrasted with a panel to create a negative effect: black marble streaked with gray.

⑤ A single panel of pale, streaked marble creates a practical and stylish backsplash behind the matching marble countertop shown here.

⑥ Streaks of pale green and blue splash the surface of these off-white marble tiles and introduce an understated pattern.

Marble floors deserve to be displayed in a broad setting, where their grandeur can be savored. Marble excels in light, airy rooms such as a glazed conservatory or a bright bathroom (especially when carried up the walls as well), and can look particularly opulent in a spacious entrance hall. Bright settings such as these will create beautiful reflections in the flooring, enhancing the freshness of the room and the beauty of the stone.

Opt for a clean look with marble in a single color or with delicate veining. Offset the subtle variations with a pure white porcelain bath and basin complete with cool chrome fittings. For a more sophisticated look, use large, mottled tiles— rich butterscotch, velvet blue, daffodil yellow with white veins, or black with gray veins—perhaps delineated with rectangular insets of cream marble. Accentuate the look with marble statues or fluted columns. When used in a bathroom, where water is present, remember that marble tiles can become slippery. Marble does have the drawback that it stains easily and will require periodic maintenance and the restoration of its seal.

① These subdued, honed marble tiles form a color link between the sections of this open-plan attic apartment.

② A basketweave design has been created here with squares of brown marble interspersed between larger beige marble tiles. The toning marble on the shower walls forges a sense of unity.

③ Streaks and flecks of white cut through the intense black of this marble flooring and bath panel, while a vivid, red-painted wall adds a sense of brooding drama.

④ Cloudy white tiles polished to a high sheen create an elegant tone to this bathroom when combined with the oak vanity unit and rich drapes.

Marble is not the easiest stone to cut into regular sheets. Mining requires careful cutting with channeling machines that cut large blocks, which are then sawn to the required shape and size. Impurities present in the limestone during recrystallization result in a wide variety of colors, from white—the purest form—to reds and browns, with other trace elements producing yellows, blues, and greens. Veining may be strong and linear or fine and gossamerlike and in darker or lighter shades than the base color. Fossil inclusions, of marine life for example, occasionally survive the formation process to produce fascinating patterns. Because veining and inclusions weaken the structure of the marble, some tiles and slabs have a mesh backing to strengthen them.

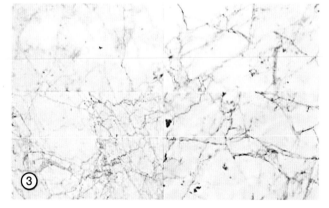

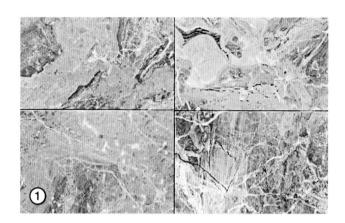

① Polished Italian beige
② Polished white
③ Polished veined white
④ Honed champagne gold
⑤ Polished cherry blossom
⑥ Polished black
⑦ Polished beige and ivory
⑧ Polished deep brown
⑨ Polished dark green
⑩ Polished jade
⑪ Polished deep green with fossil inclusions
⑫ Honed sky blue

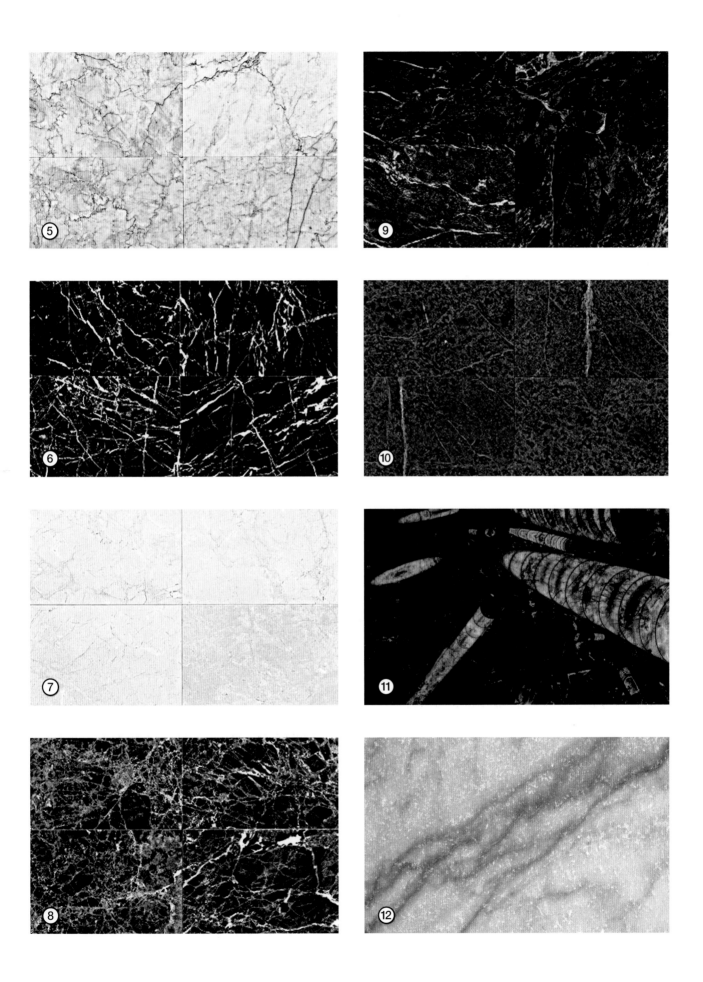

Continued from page 53.

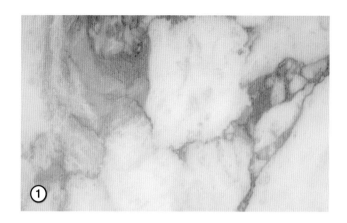

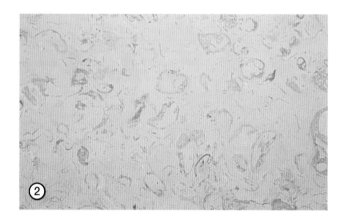

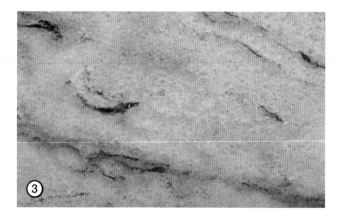

① Milk with green veining
② Off-white with fossil inclusions
③ Tumbled pink and green
④ Polished tortoiseshell filigree
⑤ Iridescent pearl
⑥ Honed green with leaf veining
⑦ Pure white, vein free
⑧ White-veined, honed crimson
⑨ Red-veined, honed gold
⑩ Polished rose and cream
⑪ Polished light and dark walnut
⑫ Honed beige with red veins

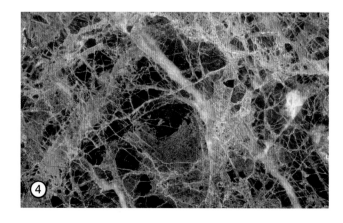

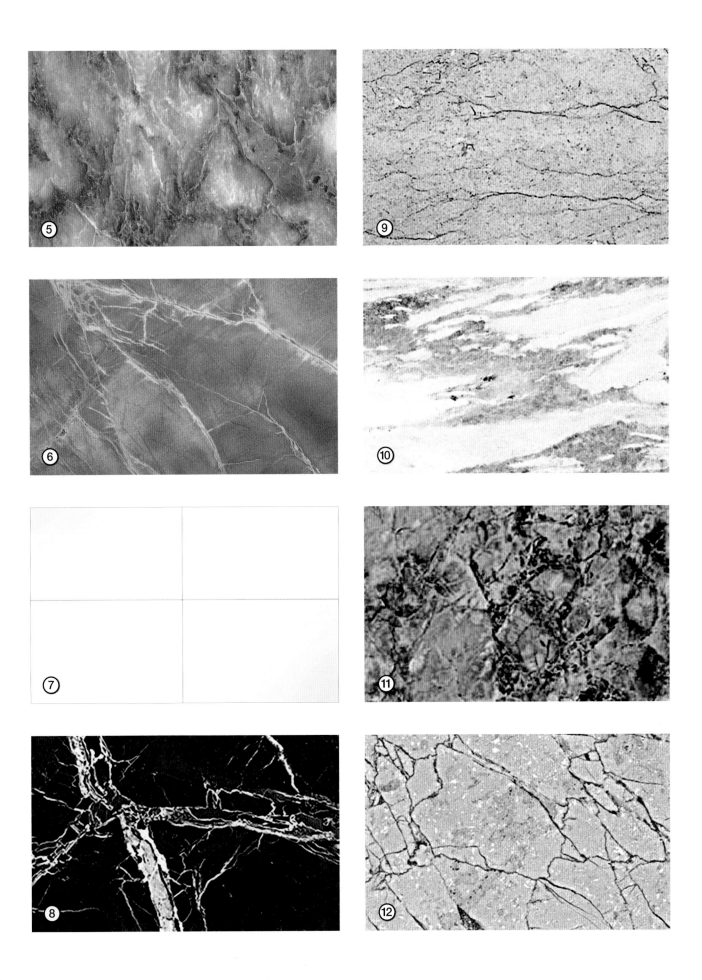

Slate and Quartzite

Slate is a dense, hard stone that has a naturally riven surface, a "natural cleft" characteristic that causes it to split into layers or sheets, making it an ideal material for creating fairly thin tiles (hence its use as a roofing and cladding material). It can, nevertheless, be honed or tumbled to provide a smoother, typically matte finish.

Quartzite, similar in appearance to slate, is one of the most durable stones—highly resistant to stains and scratching and perfect for areas subject to heavy wear and moisture. Commonly black, dark gray, greenish gray, copper, and purplish gray in color, it's a material with a dominant presence that calls for moderation.

Slate or quartzite tiles are dark and enclosing, absorbing natural light, and are therefore best reserved for focal points (such as backsplashes) rather than entire walls. Shower rooms and wet rooms are exceptions. If there is little or no natural light, wall-to-wall slate or quartzite will be dramatic in these settings. Sensitive lighting, such as ceiling-mounted, low-voltage halogen, will accentuate the riven faces of slate or create pools of subtle light on dark, honed finishes.

① Large format slate squares with minimal joints form an impervious seal against shower spray.

② Rust-colored squares of slate are arranged in a complex jigsaw pattern here, with occasional surface-fixed tiles enhancing the three-dimensional effect.

③ Slate is extremely impervious. This panel of black, honed tiles makes an imposing backsplash to the chrome shower.

④ Vertical wall planks of black, pitted quartzite, lit only by subdued artificial light, are intensely dramatic, and the perfect foil for an unusual square bidet and toilet in gleaming white porcelain.

⑤ In this bathroom, horizontal panels of quartzite with a tarnished metal appearance enhance an unusual integral glass sink with a rusted, verdigris effect.

③

⑤

④

Slate and quartzite floors are perfect for demanding rooms. The natural cleft property of slate, forming subtle surface layering, creates a practical nonslip finish, making the material one of the best choices for hard flooring, particularly in areas affected by water, such as bathrooms, shower rooms, and wet rooms. Some slate is sold as "uncalibrated," meaning that the thickness of individual units within a batch varies due to the natural cleft characteristic. When laying, this variation must be taken into account in the thickness of the adhesive bed, so that the finished surface of the tiles can be set perfectly level. Though it is a highly resistant stone, suppliers nevertheless recommend that slate be sealed to avoid scratches and other marks.

Quartzite is more standard in thickness than slate and makes for a tough and long-lasting floor with rich, powerful coloration. This type of stone is best suited to furnishings of simple lines; plain, muted, or pastel colors; and minimal pattern.

① Tumbled slate tiles in cream and red tones are arranged here in a checkerboard pattern and exude a rustic charm.

② The subtle sheen of green slate slabs accentuates the intriguing textures of this durable and attractive floor.

③ Jet-black quartzite slabs are polished to a high sheen in this floor and accentuated by stark, white grout lines.

④ Cool mint coloring is reflected onto white walls from the subtle green tinge of this slate flooring.

⑤ Slate is not always monotone—this mottled, deep-pink variety evokes a soft and sensuous warmth.

⑤

Slate is mined in many regions of the world and has been a popular variety of stone for hundreds of years. Formed from fine-grained shale (a sedimentary rock made from clay deposits that settle into layers under extreme pressure and temperature), the naturally riven or delaminated faces of slate create intriguing textures and variations in shade. Honed slate is an alternative to the riven type, but the smoothest finishes can be prone to scratch marks.

① Riven, honed silver-gray
② Honed fractured gray
③ Polished brushed green
④ Polished brushed mottled green
⑤ Honed blue and fawn
⑥ Riven cherry blossom
⑦ Riven copper
⑧ Riven silver and brown
⑨ Mottled rust
⑩ Honed multicolored
⑪ Honed light green
⑫ Riven barley

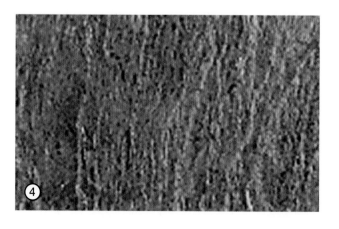

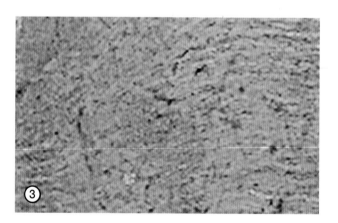

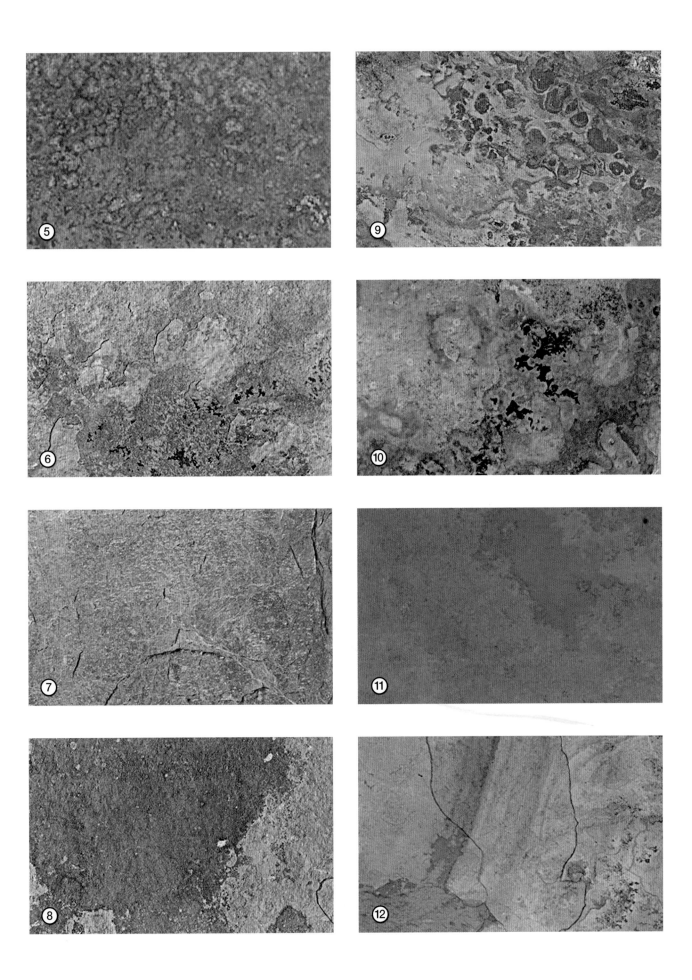

Continued from page 61.

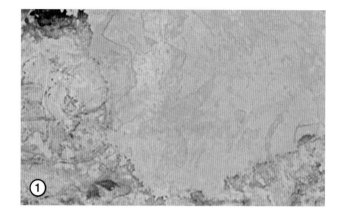

① Honed ivory and gold

② Riven lilac

③ Sanded oyster

④ Riven earth

⑤ Riven silver-gray

⑥ Tumbled green and yellow

⑦ Deeply riven gray-green

⑧ Deeply riven jade

⑨ Riven brown and gray

⑩ Riven earth

⑪ Riven gray

⑫ Riven blue-gray

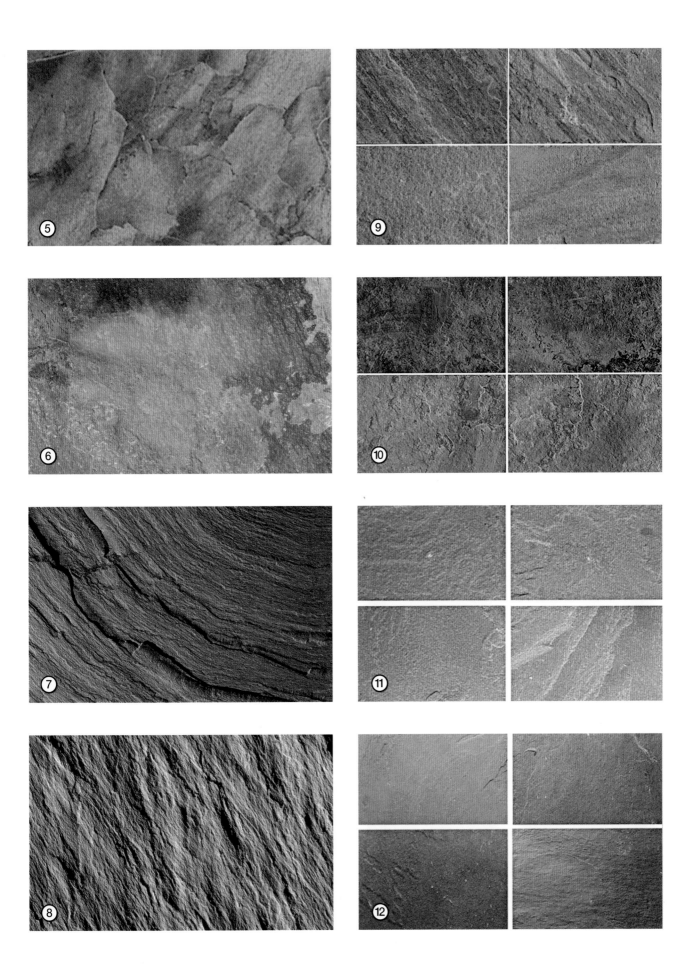

Basalt

Smooth, dark, and dramatic, basalt is best reserved for small areas such as shower cubicles, pantries (where its cool surface will create a natural chill), feature walls, or fireplaces. Some types of basalt have tiny, attractive, almond-shaped surface imperfections that were originally caused by volcanic gas bubbles when the stone was in its molten form. This type of stone is typically dark in color, commonly black, though tiles in sage green and dark purple can also be found.

① The dark character of black basalt is lightened here with sharp white grout lines, white accessories, and pure white walls and ceiling.

② Bold and uncompromising, polished basalt forms impervious walls in this master bath, where floor and walls constantly receive a good soaking.

③ Gunmetal gray basalt slabs make a practical, wipe-clean surface behind this cooker.

④ Lead-colored basalt panels line the walls of this ultra-modern bathroom, complementing a brushed aluminum shower console behind a clear glass screen.

Basalt floors are very strong. Basalt is an igneous rock—essentially solidified magma or lava—with a high density and enormous resistance to scratching and staining. Due to its coloring, a floor covered in basalt slabs or tiles will be a dominant feature that will therefore require careful furnishing to avoid creating an oppressive feel. The best type of design to accompany such a dominant stone is a minimalist, modern style. As with other dark-toned stone types, a basalt floor will also visually decrease the height of a room—a benefit for a room with high ceilings but to be avoided in rooms with low ceilings, particularly country-style period homes with heavy, exposed beams.

① Gray basalt flooring is teamed with light wood fixtures and cream paintwork here to create a clean and fresh-looking bathroom.

② Dark, mysterious, and dramatic, this black basalt flooring is matched by matte black walls and contrasted with white fixtures.

③ This honed basalt flooring acts as a subdued, solid backdrop to the exuberance of the swirling, metallic wall paneling and flamboyant chunky white fittings.

④ Modern minimalism in action: these enormous floor slabs, in light gray basalt, glow in the light coming from the glazed doorway.

④

Limestone

One of the largest stone groups, limestone is a calcareous stone with variable color and markings dependent upon its mineral content. As an architectural stone it has been used for centuries, to create structures from the Egyptian pyramids and medieval English churches to the façades of skyscrapers. A variety of limestone, Jerusalem stone is a distinctive material with a rich, golden coloring. Wall tiles cut from Jerusalem stone can have a relatively smooth honed or tumbled finish or, alternatively, rough, hand-chiseled faces.

①

②

① Gray limestone spattered with tiny pits and mineral blemishes is clean and cool, but the surface must be sealed.

② Mottled, beige limestone tiles with a honed finish create an enveloping warmth when they are used exclusively.

③ Large squares of limestone line this stairwell. The brushed finish of the tiles is alternated to add subtle texture.

④ Limestone has long been prized by sculptors: this carved panel is based on a pattern of overlapping circles.

⑤ The smooth texture of this mottled lilac limestone is relieved by an inset panel of chipped mosaic.

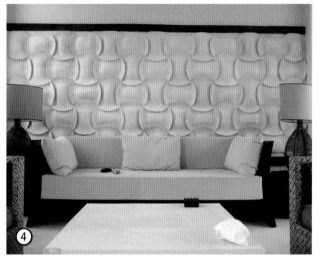

Limestone floors, compared to floors made from other stone varieties, create a less formal floor surface but still provide an elegance that complements both traditional and modern styles. As limestone is porous, hardness and density vary considerably. Sealing is required for protection against moisture and bacterial growth, especially on kitchen and bathroom floors where hygiene is important. As there is not the same degree of pitting in limestone as there is in travertine, periodic refilling is not necessary, though resealing is. The surface can be polished, honed to a matte finish, brushed, or delicately water-worn. Some degree of edge chipping should be expected, and actually enhances the aged quality of the stone.

① This pale mocha-tinted limestone is the perfect foil for the rich colors and rugged texture of the exposed stone wall.

② Muted golden limestone will draw light into a room and make the space feel larger, particularly when furnishing is understated.

③ Pale green limestone is used as a visual link between the kitchen and dining areas of this modern interior.

④ Properly sealed against moisture, limestone flooring can be used in bathrooms, as is demonstrated here. Its relative softness is easier on the feet than other stone types.

⑤ Pale pink limestone tiles help to brighten this otherwise poorly lit hallway, while ceiling-mounted halogen lamps cast pleasing pools of light.

⑥ Wall-to-wall limestone panels, allied with matching flooring, add subtle color and create a cool atmosphere.

①

②

③

⑤

④

⑥

Limestone is a sedimentary rock formed from the mineral calcite (seashells, marine organisms, and sediment) at the bottom of shallow lakes and seas. Its predominantly light coloring is influenced by the presence of minerals, such as iron oxide and dolomite, and varies from shades of white, yellow, and buff tones to gray, blue, and sometimes black. The mineral impurities produce attractive dappling, veins, flecks, and grains.

Jerusalem stone is the generic term for meleke ("royal" in Arabic), a type of dolomitic limestone quarried in the Jerusalem and Bethlehem areas of Israel. It usually has a distinctive gold or reddish hue, but some types vary from white to gray.

① Honed speckled cream
② Tumbled blue
③ Honed crabapple beige
④ Cool gray
⑤ Speckled beige
⑥ Honed ivory cream
⑦ Tumbled granular fawn
⑧ Polished ice white
⑨ Polished pale beige
⑩ Honed honey Jerusalem stone
⑪ Antique-brushed dark gray
⑫ Flame-finished gray
⑬ Black and blue swirls
⑭ Brushed black and blue
⑮ Brushed amber Jerusalem stone
⑯ Antique brushed cream

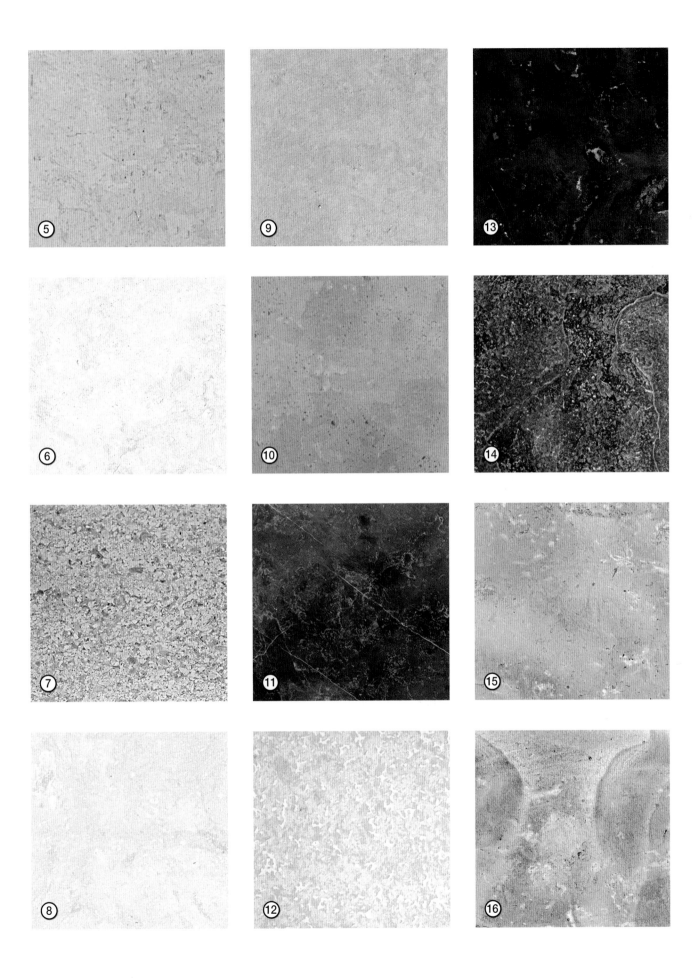

Continued from page 73.

① Honed mottled beige
② Polished with gold veins
③ Honed flax
④ Brushed blue and green
⑤ Honed gold veined
⑥ Polished gold and silver
⑦ Honed tan and gold
⑧ Polished gold
⑨ Brushed gold
⑩ Polished "Egyptian gold"
⑪ Tumbled "cloudburst"
⑫ Brushed lime green
⑬ Honed antique gold
⑭ Mottled cream
⑮ Mottled gray-blue
⑯ Polished gray with brown inclusions

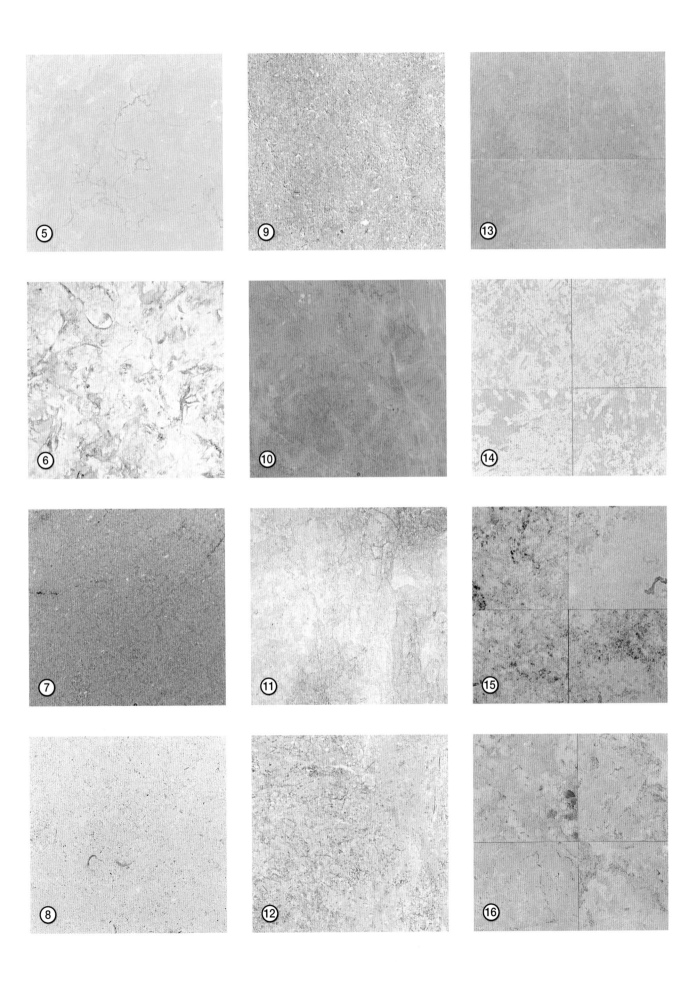

Granite

The flecked, mottled, and highly colorful surface of granite wall tile gives it a vibrant energy that can infuse a decorative scheme with a unique flavor. With such a bold character, granite is best teamed with clean, simple lines in furniture and nonpatterned fabrics to avoid visual clashes. These stone tiles require a perfectly sound and rigid base. Although units can be cut fairly thin, their combined weight and the force of gravity can cause them to separate from a weak structure. Granite tiles can easily rip a thin or poorly fixed wallboard from its supports.

① The mineral inclusions present in granite often appear to sparkle in the light, enhancing the glamorous look of this glitzy bathroom.

② These random-shaped riven granite blocks, in several contrasting tones, create a cavelike niche for showering.

③ A sunny glow bathes this lively kitchen. The effect is enhanced by the speckled, gold granite on the wall and countertop and by the pale wood fixtures.

④ Blue-gray speckled and streaked granite, polished to a mirrorlike sheen, has a distinctive, wet look when illuminated from a sun light as it is here.

①

Granite floors have many advantages. Granite is the hardest building stone, virtually impervious to water and highly resistant to wearing and chemical action. Resistance to abrasion and ease of cutting and shaping make this variety of stone a popular choice for flooring. The considerable weight of granite, however, means that the substrate must be very strong, sound, and resistant to flexing. Despite its strength, granite can fracture on a subfloor that is not completely rigid. Because of their durability, granite slabs and floor tiles are perfect for hallways, kitchens, bathrooms, and other areas of high traffic or heavy use.

②

① Mosaic inserts are used to separate these speckled granite slabs, producing a richly textured finish.

② The granular nature of granite gives these deep brown slabs a nonslip finish that also glistens in artificial light.

③ Glossy granite tiles are an ideal choice for a bathroom that is uncompromisingly sleek in style.

④ Brighten dark entrance hallways with bold colors. In this hallway, luminous, blue granite slabs in a random pattern are enlivened by the yellow glow of lighting.

Granite—from *granum*, Latin for "grain"—is a form of igneous rock and is extremely hard, with a crystalline structure rather than the layered structure of sedimentary rock. It contains traces of feldspar, quartz, mica, and other minerals in pronounced flecks. The stone can be worked to a soft sheen or a highly mirrored finish, and its phenomenal range of hues and textural patterns—along with its consistency of color and texture—make it one of the most popular and decorative of stone varieties. Base colors are characteristically mottled in shades of white, brown, yellow, pink, green, blue, gray, and black, with contrasting flecks that invest it with an almost three-dimensional depth. Major sources of granite include Scandanavia, Portugal, Spain, Brazil, and India.

① Polished gold
② Deep cream
③ Almond and mauve
④ Red speckled
⑤ Black galaxy
⑥ Blue star
⑦ Tortoiseshell
⑧ Mottled cream
⑨ Green diamond
⑩ Lavender blue
⑪ Chrysanthemum yellow
⑫ Peach
⑬ Speckled gold
⑭ Mottled brown
⑮ Tree bark
⑯ Cloudy gray

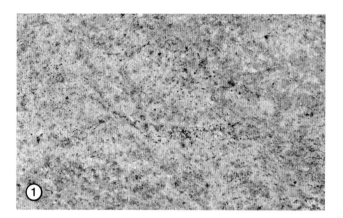

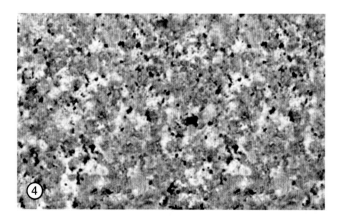

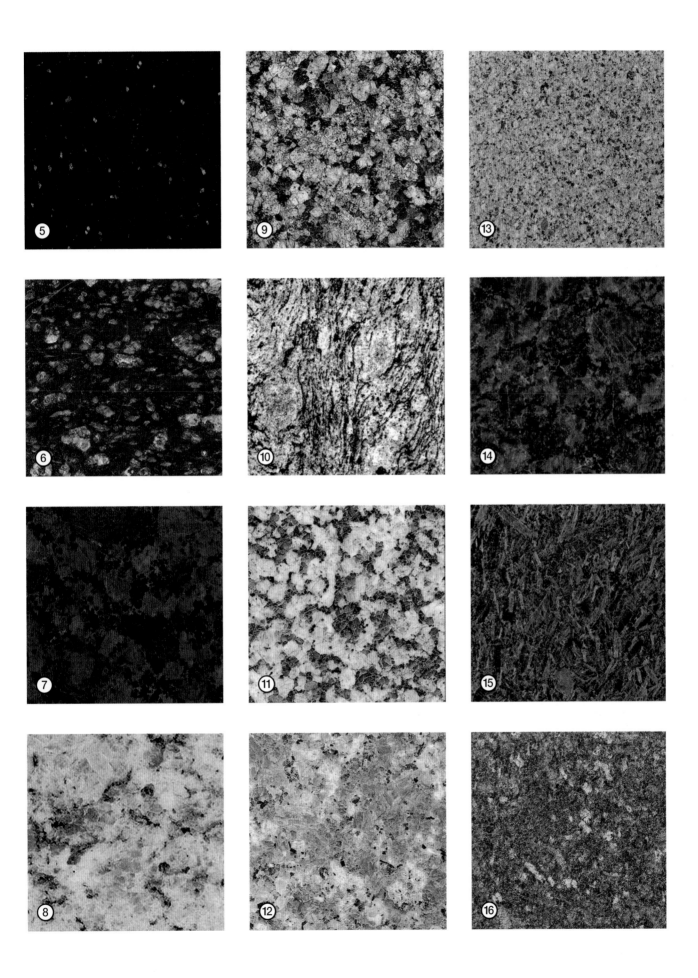

Continued from page 81.

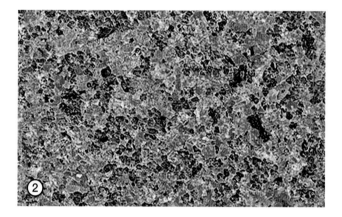

① Brown and sapphire
② Snow plum
③ Jade
④ Moss green
⑤ Streaked violet
⑥ Powder pink
⑦ Rust red
⑧ Tiger red
⑨ Cream and mauve
⑩ Wave white
⑪ Speckled pearl white
⑫ Honed gold
⑬ Ruby red
⑭ Bright pink
⑮ Night sky
⑯ Rust and black

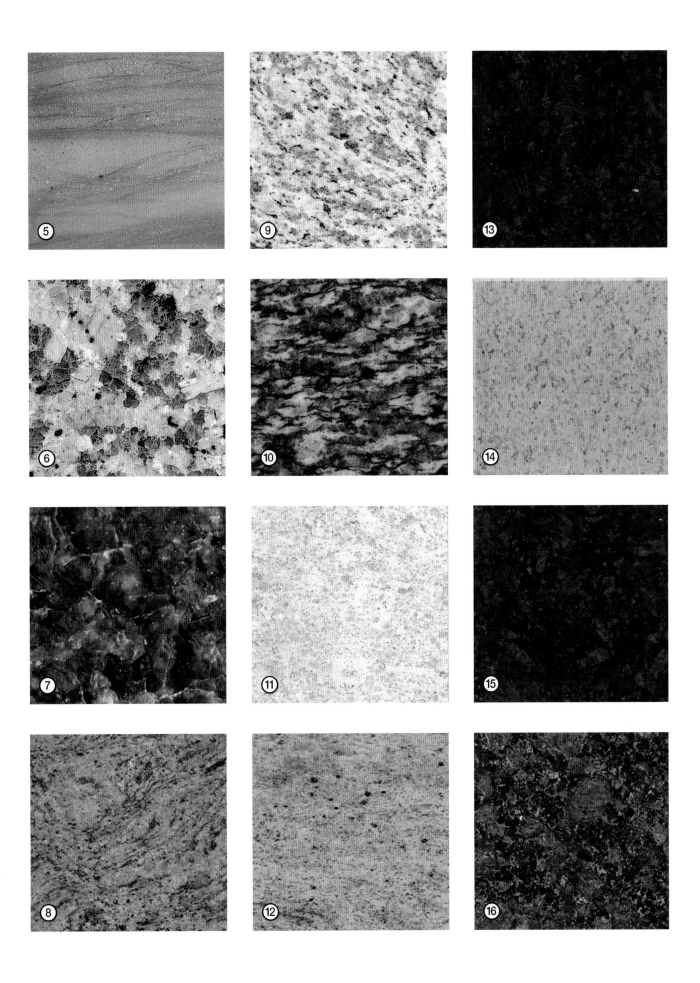

Sandstone

Sandstone wall tiles are available in a wonderful array of natural, earthy tones and delicate pastels. They have a softness and surface texture that harks back to their origins—compressed sand, minerals, and earth—and which makes them superb for adding color and fine texture to your walls. Rows of small tiles with broad, colored mortar joints make a fine backdrop for a scheme incorporating dainty floral-patterned fabric drapes and upholstery. Larger tiles with thin grout lines give a broader area of color and fine texture. Honed finishes will enhance the color, while riven faces will be more subtle in tone but display the stone's granular finish.

① The sundrenched color and texture of the beach has been brought indoors thanks to the grainy sandstone tiling shown here.

② A faux chimney in pale yellow sandstone, highlighted by duck egg-blue walls, adds a sense of scale to this room and contrasts with the terra-cotta flooring.

③ The soft pastel tones, plain fabrics, and subtle, natural textures of this living room are unified by the riven-faced sandstone tiles cladding the fireplace.

④ The warm yet contemporary feel of this bathroom is largely created by the pitted sandstone walls, which complement the modern sinks and glass shelving.

⑤ Sandstone fragments are embedded in a sand-colored mortar base in this dining room, to create the impression of an exposed stone wall.

①

Sandstone floors are ubiquitous in period style homes, particularly country-style kitchens with features such as woodburning stoves, oak ceilings and wall beams, pine furniture, and dried flower displays. If you want to achieve this old-fashioned effect, install sandstone flooring in the form of large, riven-faced slabs. Smoother, more regular floor slabs with a honed finish suit conservatories and rooms that receive a lot of natural light, creating a lustrous glow. The less rustic forms best complement modern furniture.

① Tumbled sandstone slabs provide a cool floor surface. They blend well with brushed steel work surfaces in this modern kitchen.

② Sandstone slabs are a practical solution for a bathroom or spa room (as shown here) because their riven faces provide a nonslip finish.

③ Large, square, smooth-honed sandstone slabs emphasize the geometric theme of the fittings and furnishings in this contemporary interior, while adding subtle color.

④ Rustic sandstone slabs mirror the richness in the coloring of old pine furniture, and provide the perfect match for country-style décor.

⑤ Sandstone can be prematurely aged by tumbling, which produces an instant antiqued look like this.

⑥ The natural light streaming through these windows allows the sandstone to glow, highlighting its fascinating patina.

Sandstone is a coarse-grained sedimentary rock formed by compressed grains of sand deposited by water or wind. River beds, ocean beaches, and sand dunes will all one day become sandstone. Sandstone has a granular surface and is hard yet porous, requiring thorough impregnation and surface sealing for interior use. Color ranges reflect the shades of the native sand from which it is formed, but broadly include red, pink, yellow, tan, gray, and white. The characteristics of sandstone are similar to those of limestone, but sandstone is cheaper, making it a popular choice for flooring. For areas that receive heavy traffic, honed finishes are most suitable: polished surfaces show wear more quickly; and honed finishes can tolerate more rigorous cleaning.

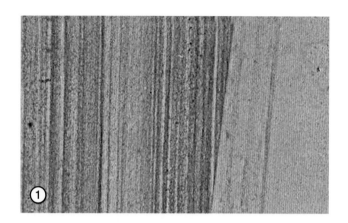

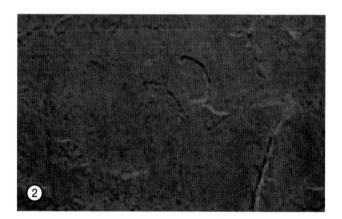

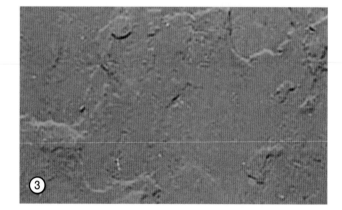

① Polished teak
② Riven chocolate
③ Natural red
④ Natural vanilla with fossil
⑤ Natural pink
⑥ Natural gray
⑦ Natural yellow
⑧ Riven desert
⑨ Polished gold with gray streaks
⑩ Natural lilac
⑪ Honed pale cream
⑫ Honed yellow streaked
⑬ Honed mahogany
⑭ Honed pale walnut
⑮ Polished, riven beige
⑯ Polished plum

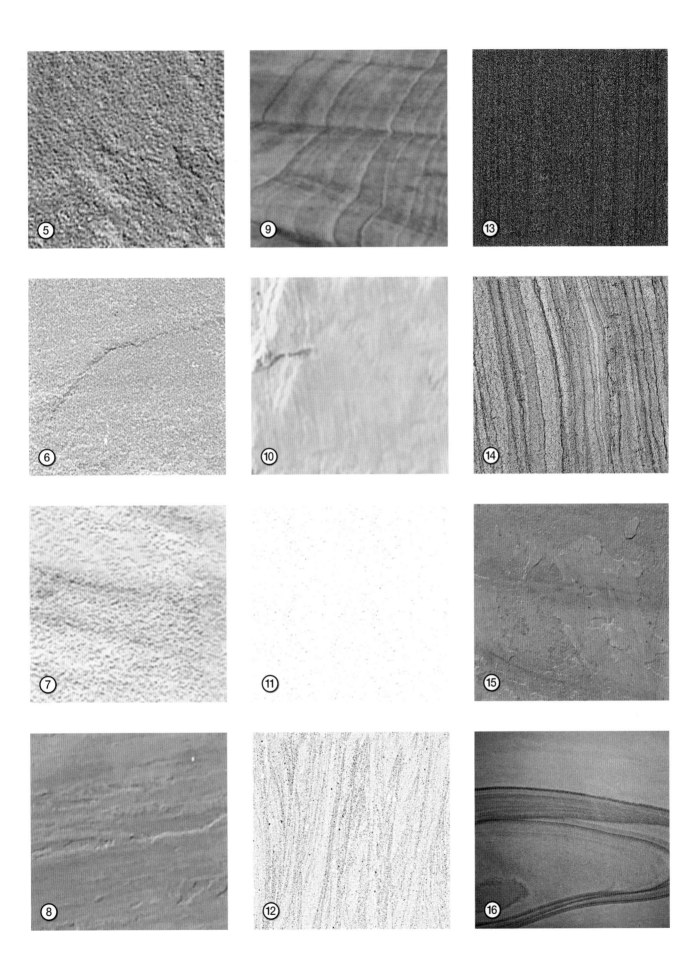

Continued from page 89.

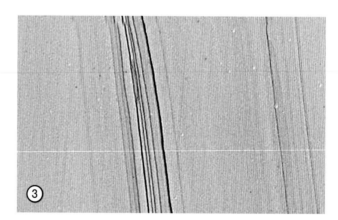

① Riven plum
② Riven deep red
③ Polished peach, with streaks
④ Natural brown
⑤ Natural gold
⑥ Natural coral
⑦ Honed yellow
⑧ Natural earth
⑨ Tumbled wheat
⑩ Tumbled beige
⑪ Tumbled mauve
⑫ Polished brown with inclusions
⑬ Honed light brown
⑭ Honed butterscotch
⑮ Polished desert
⑯ Riven terra-cotta

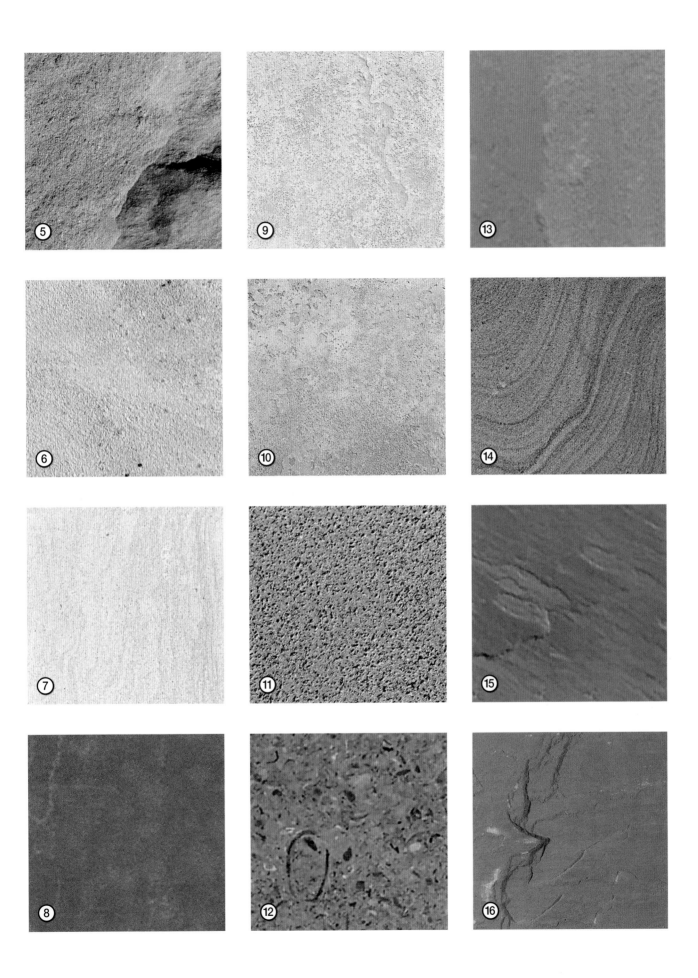

Mosaic

A mosaic is a picture or pattern created by arranging small pieces of different colored tile. The individual tiles—known as *tesserae* to the Greeks and Romans, who are renowned in the art of creating mosaics—are bedded in mortar and the multitude of joints grouted, either flush with the surface or recessed. Tiles are now also available attached to a flexible mesh backing, forming a larger set that can be stuck to the surface with special adhesive. Mosaics can be applied to walls, used to clad surfaces such as bath panels and vanity units, and even wrapped around columns.

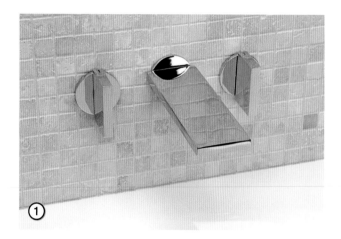

① Pink and cream travertine with a tumbled finish add subtle texture and color to this contemporary scheme.

② When using mosaics wall to wall, and across the entire floor, it's best to use mesh-backed tiles, such as the random arrangements of pale blue and white limestone tesserae shown here.

③ A maritime theme works well in bathrooms. These dark green quartz tiles provide an oceanic feel, helping to bring a sense of tranquility to a cluttered space.

④ Highly polished mosaic tiles have been used to create tone-in-tone stripes on the walls and floor to create the sense of a large space.

⑤ Mosaics need not be brightly colored, a single tone such as this rosy beige can create an understated elegance.

⑥ Murals such as this delicately colored example might be laid according to a manufacturer's plan or by following a design of your own.

Mosaic floors need careful consideration: bear in mind that an entire floor laid with small-scale mosaics may appear too busy and render any pattern indistinct. Consider how you might use the tiles in moderation as a border or inlay. If you are creating a pictorial mosaic on a floor, it should ideally be positioned centrally, for greatest impact. In a bathroom or shower stall, the many grout joints of a mosaic—apart from forming a vital element of the design—can be beneficial as they help to provide a nonslip finish.

① These gray mosaic tiles, attached to a mesh backing, are flexible enough to be carried around a curve, softening the join between wall and floor.

② Black squares framed by white rectangles create an intricate swirl pattern here, which picks up on the black of the washstand.

③ These streaky beige floor tiles tone with the larger wall tiles while still offering a variation in texture.

④ Colorful geometric designs like this one can be obtained as a kit of parts or as prefabricated panels.

⑤ Different shades of stone fragments create interesting shapes and contrasts on these mosaic-covered steps.

⑥ These mosaic tiles create a random effect, but they have been orientated to avoid a concentration of color. Ceramic tiles around the bathroom fittings provide contrast.

⑦ This flamboyant beach appearance has been created with polished, rounded stones that imitate seaside pebbles. A whirlpool design on the floor finishes the effect.

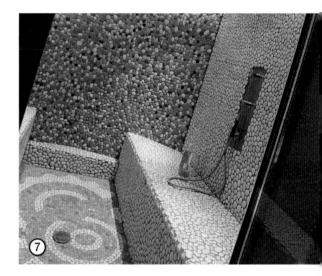

Mosaic tiles can create designs that are geometric, pictorial, abstract, or even single-colored, for an effect is more textural than pattern-based. Mesh-backed tiles enable you to cover large areas quickly and are composed of single colors, random or geometric patterns, or pictorial designs. Not all tesserae are squares; individual pieces, or those contained in backed tiles, may be octagonal, rectangular, rounded, or even irregularly shaped.

① Grouted tan hexagons and diamonds
② Grouted gray hexagons and diamonds
③ Grouted tiles in tumbled gray
④ Cream, gray, and gold tiles with wide joints
⑤ Cream and gray tiles with wide joints
⑥ Rust and cream tiles with wide joints
⑦ Grouted gray and cream tumbled
⑧ Grouted mottled tan tumbled
⑨ Grouted tiles in classic checkerboard
⑩ Grouted white rectangles around black squares
⑪ Grouted tiles in shades of blue and white
⑫ Grouted tiles in shades of brown
⑬ Grouted tiles with two sizes of squares
⑭ Grouted tiles in fawn
⑮ Grouted tiles in chestnut
⑯ Grouted tiles in mottled white
⑰ Grouted contrasting hexagons and squares
⑱ Grouted tiles in golden yellow
⑲ Grouted tiles in ocean gray
⑳ Backed tiles in light tan

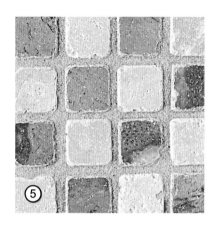

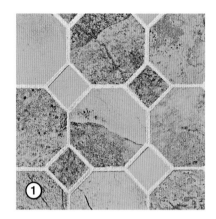

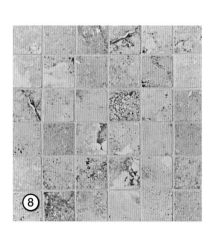

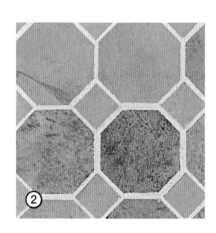

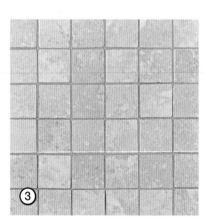

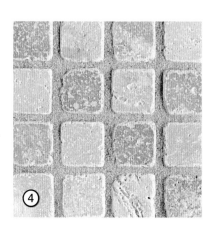

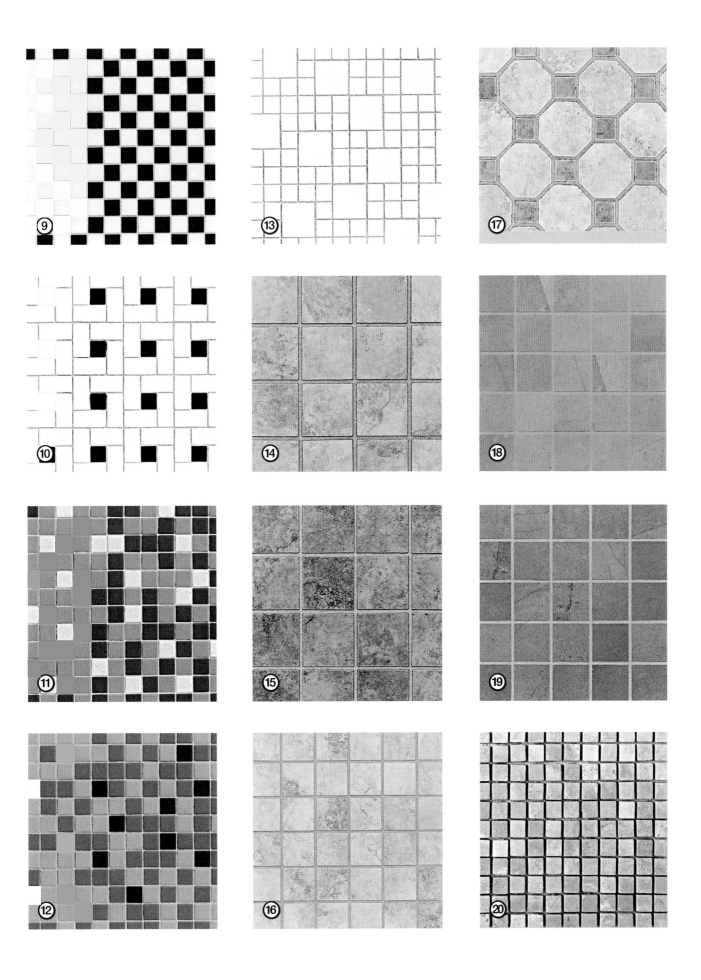

Continued from page 97.

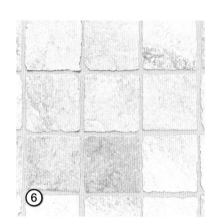

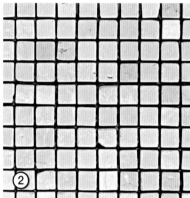

① Backed tiles in rust
② Backed tiles in off-white
③ Backed tiles in gray marble
④ Backed tiles in clay brown
⑤ Backed tiles in jade
⑥ Grouted tiles in mottled chalk
⑦ Grouted tiles in gray-brown
⑧ Grouted tiles in ivory
⑨ Grouted tiles in pale green
⑩ Grouted tiles in two-tone buff
⑪ Grouted tiles in peach
⑫ Grouted tiles in brown and deep pink
⑬ Backed tiles in tumbled sandstone
⑭ Backed tiles in burnt sugar
⑮ Grouted tiles in speckled gray, brown, and cream
⑯ Grouted tiles in tawny shades
⑰ Grouted tiles in pale biscuit
⑱ Grouted tiles in pale orange
⑲ Grouted tiles in walnut
⑳ Grouted, tumbled tiles in pale sand, with wide joints

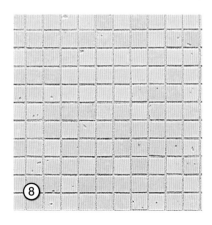

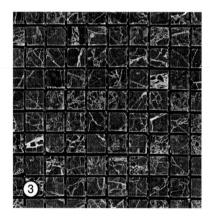

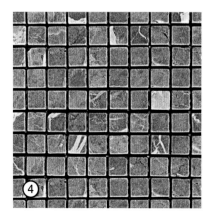

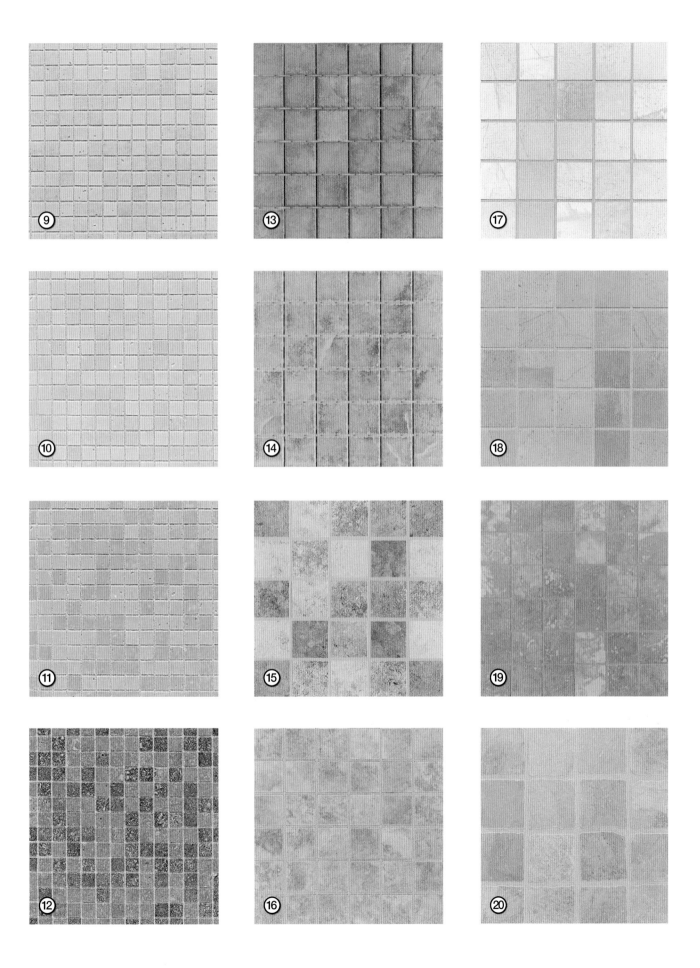

Patterns for Floors

The size and shape of individual tiles or slabs, and the way you position them on the floor, will significantly affect the visual proportions of a room. With careful planning, you can use this effect to your advantage.

When planning flooring, bear in mind that, in general, the larger the room the larger the slab you will be able to use. Large slabs used in small rooms not only waste stone, because you would have to make more cuts, but also do not allow them to show their best qualities. Smaller slabs or tiles will make a room seem bigger, but choose plain types to avoid too frenetic a scheme.

Square, plain-edged slabs laid edge to edge in a checkerboard pattern create a grid that is best suited to more formal settings. Emphasize the grid effect by laying lines of narrow rectangular tiles, or even rows of mosaics, between the slabs. Rectangular units laid parallel to the longer dimension of a room create the impression that it is longer than it really is. Conversely, rectangular slabs laid parallel to the shorter dimension of a room appear to shorten it.

Staggering the joints half a slab's length between each row creates a less formal "running bond," often used in brickwork, while combining square and rectangular tiles breaks up a uniform grid. Taken one step further, using a mix of several sizes and shapes of slab fitted together jigsaw fashion creates a random, informal pattern on the floor. More complex laying patterns can be achieved by laying rectangular units in a zigzagging herringbone, basketweave, or parquet design. Even setting the area of tile diagonally to the walls will create an interesting, jaunty effect.

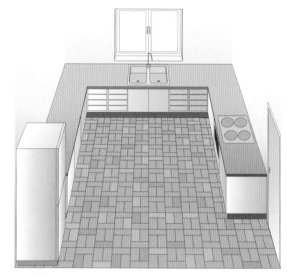

Basketweave

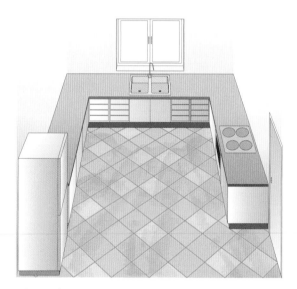

Diagonal

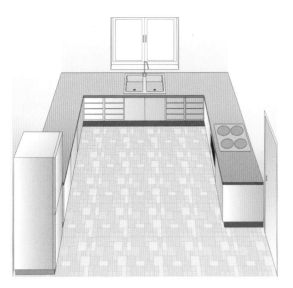

French random

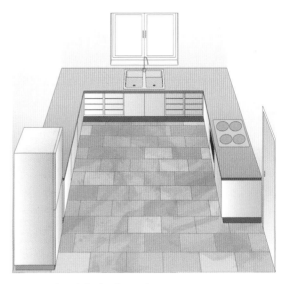

Rectangular slabs horizontal

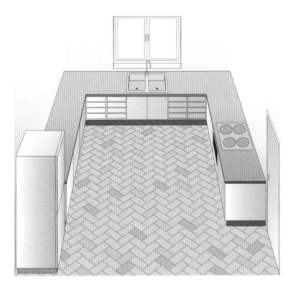

Herringbone

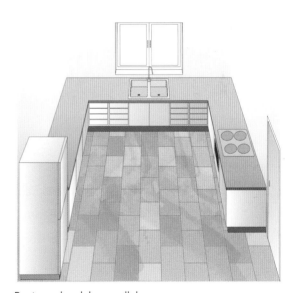

Rectangular slabs parallel

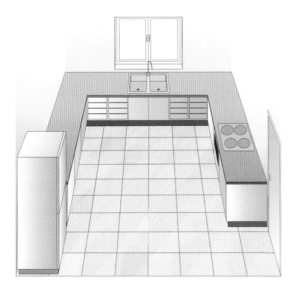

Large slabs

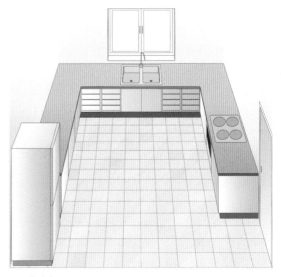

Small slabs

Color and Texture for Floors

While the sizes and shapes of floor tiles or slabs influence the proportions of a room, color and texture also play an important role. A single color of blue slate tiles laid on a checkerboard grid with stark white grout lines is smart and sophisticated; black, diamond-shaped insets fitted at the corners of white marble slabs create a classic, geometric effect; while weathered, riven-faced sandstone slabs evoke an old-world, rural look.

A single color of slabs or tiles, particularly lighter toned stone, will give a cool sense of space, while a simple checkerboard pattern using two colors—white and black, cream and green, or blue and yellow—can form a backdrop for your furnishings. Pick out toning colors in upholstery, drapes, or even paintings or other decorative touches.

If you're using strong, dominant colors for flooring, however, it's best to contrast this with a more neutral treatment in the color of kitchen units, sofas, and other furnishings. There's no reason why you can't combine several colors in one floor, though this would result in a vibrant scheme perhaps more suited to a fun bathroom or lively games room than a relaxing living room.

Also consider how you can alternate polished stones and those with a matte finish. Combine rustic, riven tiles with smooth honed types, or use glossy, granular granite slabs as an inset in an area of honed limestone.

Barred square

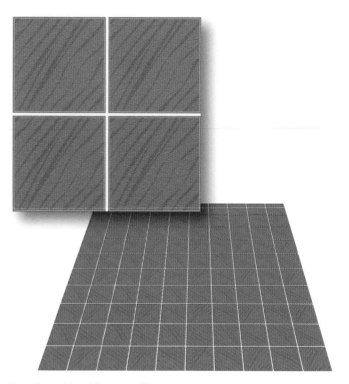

Blue tiles with white grout lines

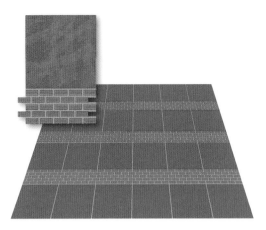

Square tiles with inset strip of rectangular mosaics

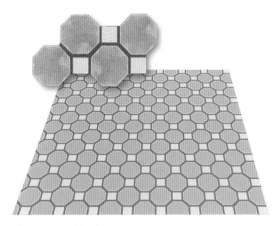

Octagons with dots

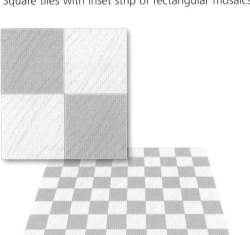

Cream and green checkerboard

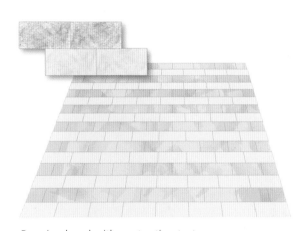

Running bond with contrasting textures

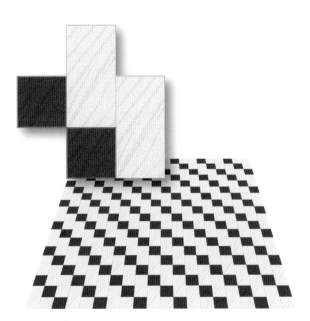

Diagonal pattern

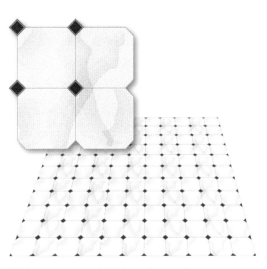

White octagons with black diamonds

Color and Patterns for Walls

The same patterns used for floors can also be used for laying stone wall tiles, with similar effects on the proportion of the room. The main difference is generally scale: patterns comprised of large tiles will make a wall too dominant, whereas smaller tiles will be more delicate and less overwhelming. As with flooring, consider mixing and matching colors in patterns such as checkerboard, basketweave, and running bonds, and combining polished and matte tiles. Dramatic results can also be achieved by introducing panels of mosaic or by stenciling or painting onto stone tiles, using a highly colorful palette of penetrating stone glazes.

Pinwheel

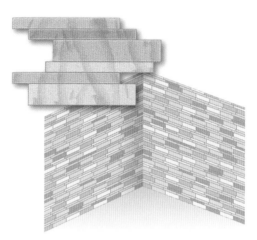

Running bond in thin, rectangular tiles

Alternating checkerboard

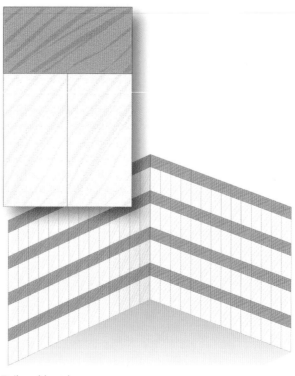

Railroad bond

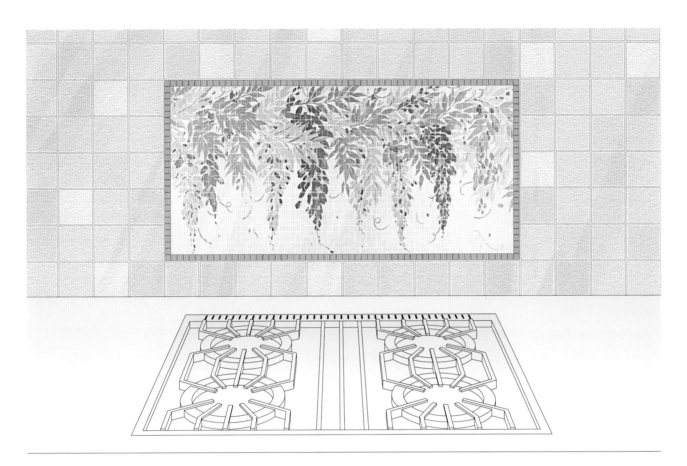

Mosaic mural on backsplash

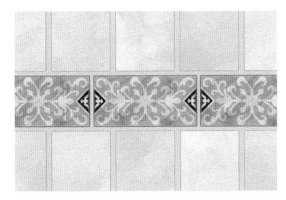

Decorative line inset

Diamond tiles with white grout lines

Mixed colors and shapes in random positions

Interior Decorative Stonework

Stone tiles and slabs are attractive and practical additions to your home décor, but you can also use stonework for its purely aesthetic qualities, by adding accessories such as Corinthian columns, moldings, and stone architraves to complement a scheme, or by incorporating ornamental urns, statues, plaques, and objets d'art into your designs.

Antique shops, auctions, and architectural salvage yards are useful sources of decorative items in real stone that you can use to embellish your home. Stone columns with Doric capitals, ornate urns, finials, and classical statues can form the basis of a Romanesque bathroom, for example; particularly when teamed with marble wall and floor tiles or pictorial murals. Suppliers of garden ornaments even produce hollow, lightweight columns, lintels, and other architectural components in reconstituted limestone, cast in original molds for authenticity.

Classical busts and obelisks on pedestals can also give a grand appearance to an entrance hallway, while pedestals make the perfect display vehicles for potted plants, glass, or chinaware and can provide support for a glass or marble tabletop. Low stone pilasters make fine occasional tables, while balusters and handrails can be used as divisions within rooms.

The look of stone quoins, or cornerstones, can be imitated by placing staggered blocks around a doorway or as a feature on an otherwise plain wall. Similarly, a stonework architrave can be fixed around a doorway to create a grand entrance. Dado rails cut from real stone, or molded from reconstituted stone, will add a stylish touch to a

dining room. Consider using stone path or lawn edging as an indoor skirt in the angle between floor and wall, perhaps in conjunction with matching stone tiles or slabs. A decorative stone plaque set within a wall is a tactile alternative to the ubiquitous framed painting.

In a living room, an elegant stone fire surround and hearth creates a warming focal point. Select from a huge range of different styles, from period to ultra modern.

Carry through the stonework theme with a simple, elegant stonework objet d'art. Small statuettes, animal carvings, fossils, and even collections of colorful beach stones make interesting decorative displays. Consider refining your collection to a specific theme by collecting semi-precious gemstones or the popular and intriguing stone eggs that are found all over the world. Eggs formed from numerous stone varieties, in wonderful colors and fascinating textures and patterns, are sought after by many people to be displayed in a bowl or arranged on a shelf.

In the kitchen, a stone pestle and mortar, used for crushing herbs and spices, makes a stylish and useful addition to your cooking equipment (don't hide it in a cupboard!), while original stone sinks—or modern equivalents for outdoor use—can provide a period touch in a rustic home.

Opposite: Stone sculptures, either hand-carved or cast in molds, stir the imagination. A monkey climbs a stylized tree here for drama on a large scale.

Below: The stone sconce and candlestick holder in this bathroom are exhibited to wonderful effect against simple white.

Interior Architectural Features

When choosing architectural stonework for indoors, think of the prevailing styles of the period or region you want to re-create. Three types of column derive from Greek architecture: oldest and simplest, the Doric has a fluted column and smooth, rounded "capital" (a broader section) at the top; the Ionic, with a rounded base, has characteristic scrolled capitals; the Corinthian has a rounded base and features olive, laurel, or acanthus leaf decoration on the capital. Egyptian columns taper out at the top and are often ornamented with palm leaves; whereas Romanesque columns are often square and squat, with trapezoidal bases and floral capital decorations.

Door surrounds comprising half-columns, pilasters, and flat or pitched entablatures can often be made up from standard components sold by cast stone manufacturers. Some types incorporate 18th-century fluting, dentil moldings, elaborate carving, and ornate capitals.

① The dressed stonework and arched panel of this Renaissance bedroom provides the room with a fitting regal elegance.

② Introduce cast stone as a sculptural feature, and there is no limit to what you can create. A rock-face effect carries the force of nature into this idiosyncratic hallway.

③ Pristine white marble balusters and rails against rich red walls suggest a dwelling of distinction. Without these features the setting would be plain.

④ An austere medieval style is re-created here with exposed stone walls and a dressed stone niche, which has been put to good use as a bookshelf.

⑤ Egyptian-style square columns such as these can be assembled from hollow stone pilasters, with stone slabs as the capitals.

⑥ As well as adding a touch of grandeur, columns can be used to divide a space or to draw focus toward a feature wall, like the one in this opulent sitting room.

⑦ An eclectic mix of styles that work well together: an Art Deco fire surround flanked by twin obelisks and a classical plaque of griffins.

Stone Ornaments

Choosing ornamental stonework is largely a matter of personal taste—you may be drawn by the classically beautiful or the quirky. The main criteria is that it should complement your overall scheme. An ornament may be a simple, aesthetically pleasing pile of smooth, white stones arranged in the corner of a sunny bathroom, as if brought in from the beach, a finely carved statue or bust mounted on a plinth, a rugged block of stone with primitive carvings or embedded fossils, or a stone garden urn doubling as a plant holder or party-time drinks cooler.

① An elegant sandstone fireplace and small, carved figurine create a scene of understated adornment.

② Use stone as a theme to create a display of disparate ornaments, such as the imposing granite wheel and assorted figurines shown here.

③ The linear shapes of these sleek modern bathroom fittings are softened by a tray of smooth round stones surrounding the bath.

④ A novel jardinière in yellow lombok fossil stone makes a fine centerpiece to this corner display of houseplants.

⑤ A large block of carved black granite forms the basis of a novel water feature in this spa room.

⑥ Choose a peice of stone sculpture to bring art into your home. Carved wooden panels form the backdrop to a cast limestone piece in this feature corner.

Stone ornaments will bring both color and texture to your home décor. An unpolished, gritty sandstone figurine, for example, would probably be most at home in rustic surroundings, while the highly polished, smooth marble bust of a historical figure is perhaps more appropriate in a traditional, formal setting. There are no strict rules because an eclectic mix of styles might be just right for your personal tastes. Searching for and finding that special ornamental item is an adventure in itself.

① Sandstone Buddha head
② Cherub head
③ Modern sandstone head
④ Ornate carved sconce
⑤ Ionic "ram's head" scrolled capital; fluted column
⑥ Corinthian capital with scrollwork and foliage; fluted column
⑦ Fish fossil in limestone block
⑧ Ammonite fossils
⑨ A freestanding sandstone fountain with pebbles that conceal a small pump to circulate water
⑩ Carved bust of Lord Byron on fluted column
⑪ Planter in cast limestone
⑫ Stone maidens on a birdbath used as an indoor planter

⑤

⑥

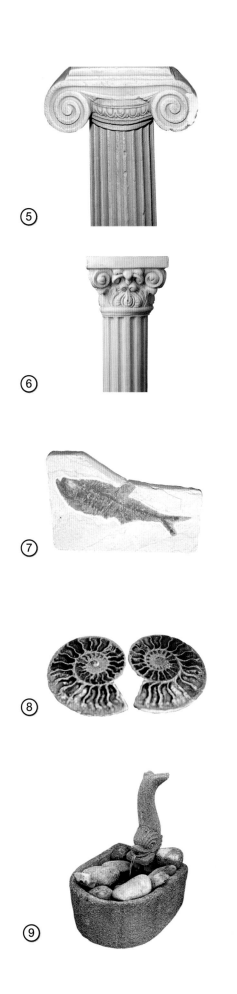

⑦

⑧

⑨

⑩

⑪

⑫

Continued from page 113.

① Marble bust of Greek godess
② Hand study in carved limestone
③ Abstract love in white marble
④ Mother and child statue in
   carved pink sandstone
⑤ Carved white marble plaque
⑥ Elephant-headed Hindu god
   Ganesh in a carved plaque
⑦ Standing Buddha statue with bowl
   in carved sandstone
⑧ Bamboo plaque in cast limestone

⑤

⑦

⑥

⑧

Stone Fittings

Sweeping innovations in 21st-century domestic design have relegated standard porcelain bathroom fittings, stainless steel kitchen sinks, wooden countertops, and plastic baths to the past and brought to the fore materials from prehistory. Stone is now crafted into sleek, stylish, and beautiful fittings that totally transform the way we think about kitchens and bathrooms. Elsewhere, traditional stonework fittings such as fire surrounds have survived the introduction of central heating and reemerged as the warming focal point of a room. In the hallway, stone is now seen as a sophisticated alternative to the conventional wooden staircase.

For many years we have come to accept the modern-day, almost universal standardization of kitchen and bathroom fittings, sacrificing our imaginations when it comes to design and aesthetics. The mass production of pressed steel kitchen sinks and molded plastic baths has largely been to blame, and choice has been very limited. Specialist companies still offer exciting ranges in these materials, but at a premium price.

Now, however, stone—an age-old resource hewn from the earth—has been adopted as a thoroughly modern and versatile material. Technology has advanced so that the raw material can be delicately cut, intricately shaped, and finely finished in numerous ways that enhance its inherent beauty. Various finishing treatments can now improve the suitability of stone in areas such as the kitchen, where durability, hygiene, and practicality are essential, and in the bathroom, where surfaces need to be impervious.

Synthetic and plastic laminate countertops are undeniably hardy, but granite—second only to diamond in hardness—will not blister, scratch, or crack and is highly stain resistant and naturally beautiful.

While many stone countertops, baths, and basins are indeed cut and shaped from slabs or blocks of natural stone, others sold as "quartz surfaces,"

"stone composite," or "engineered stone," are blended (not 100 percent solid stone). An example of quartz composite might be made up of 93 percent quartz aggregate and 7 percent pigments and polymers. The resulting mixture is then compacted by vacuum and pressure into slabs or molded and kiln cured until they possess true stone properties, but with greater long-term performance and higher resistance to stains and impact. These stone-based materials are every bit as relevant as genuine stone products, generally cheaper, and often available with finer edge profiles, detailing, and molded sections than solid stone material is able to offer.

Composite stone fittings also have numerous benefits over their natural cousins. Molded items will be much lighter than the equivalent solid versions, and it's said by some that a composite stone bath will retain the heat of the water for longer than a natural stone version.

Fire surrounds can also either be carved from natural stone or made from reconstituted stone—cast in hand-carved molds so that they look and feel real. Stair components, too, come shaped from the real thing or assembled from cast stone products. Both of these methods will create a feature that adds beauty and substance to your home.

Opposite: Fireplaces form the focal point of a room. The sensuous lines of this Art Nouveau style surround fulfills that function—whether the fire is lit or not.

Below: The honed sheen of this slate kitchen countertop is highly durable, stain and scratch resistant, and a natural partner to stained wood units.

Types and Sizes

Stone for countertops and vanity units is commonly sold per square foot, with each square foot weighing about 25 to 30 pounds (11.3–13.6 kg), depending on thickness. Thickness is relative to the size of the slab: the larger the slab, the thicker it must be to ensure its rigidity and to lessen the risk of cracking. Slabs of granite, marble, and slate are typically 10 feet (3 m) long, 26 inches (66 cm) wide, and between ½ to 2 inches (1.5–5 cm) thick; soapstone slabs are generally smaller, measuring 4 x 2 feet (120 x 60 cm).

Vanity unit countertops are narrower than kitchen slabs, often 22 inches (56 cm) wide. Silicone bead seams are needed between lengths and on L-shaped sections to accommodate the natural expansion and contraction of the stone due to temperature changes. The seams—about ¹⁄₁₆ inch (2 mm) wide—are usually visible on the multicolored and lighter granite countertops. Some manufacturers supply prefabricated countertops in sizes of about 25½ x 96 inches (65 x 243 cm) and countertops for island units 36 x 76 inches and 42 x 84 inches (91.5 x 193 cm and 106.5 x 213 cm). Countertops can be made with profiled edges—typically bullnosed, double bullnosed, rounded, beveled, or chamfered—and may feature an optional matching backsplash.

Stonework baths, basins, and other sanitaryware are made in a range of styles in nonstandard dimensions.

Stonework staircases are generally made in custom sizes to suit the specific situation, though step and tread dimensions conform to normal standards to ensure safe, trip-free use. Dimensions that need to be taken into account are the "run" (the horizontal distance between the face of the

first and last risers) and the "rise" (the vertical distance between the floors or landings connected by the flight).

Stonework fireplaces are made in a wide variety of nonstandard prefabricated sizes and can also be custom made to suit specific locations.

① This limestone vanity unit features a backward sloping basin that empties into a full-width slot at the back.

② Soft tones belie even the toughness of stone, and this luxury bathroom proves the point. A sumptuous bath sculpted from pink, almost soaplike, travertine is set against the deep pink marble of the walls and floor to exude warmth.

③ Honed—and nonslip—limestone steps lead down into this spacious indoor pool.

④ Introduce a touch of period elegance to any room with cast limestone fixtures such as this Gothic fire surround, which houses a cast iron woodburning stove.

⑤ A glossy granite island unit with an inset sink reflects light from the dramatic black chandelier overhead, creating the illusion of greater space in this grand open-plan room.

⑥ Pale colored marble, such as this delicate honed beige, has a fresh look that is clean and bright in a modern kitchen, reflecting and enhancing the natural light of the room.

Countertops and Vanities

Kitchen countertops and vanity unit surfaces are available in a range of stone varieties, each with particular characteristics and degrees of durability and impermeability.

Granite is the most popular stone type for kitchens. An extremely hard material, it is highly resistant to impact, scratching, and staining but does require regular cleaning, polishing, and sealing. The darker granites—notably those from the Middle East—are generally harder than lighter colors, which are slightly more susceptible to staining because of their mineral content.

Quartz is one of the hardest minerals. A countertop of this stone will be highly resistant to permanent staining from wine, lemon juice, fruits, vegetables, soda, and tea—all of which can harm granite and other stones.

Slate is one of the most durable stones for withstanding heavy kitchen use, and it is also popular for bathroom surfaces. A low-maintenance stone, slate requires only periodic application of mineral oil sealer. Slate is unaffected by hot pots and pans, and has natural stain resistance—minor damage can usually be polished out.

Soapstone, largely composed of the mineral talc, is unaffected by the acid and alkaline compounds that damage granite, marble, and slate. It is also highly durable under longterm kitchen and bathroom use.

Marble is one of the softer stones used for countertops and vanity unit surfaces and will require extra care to maintain its exquisite beauty. It is easily scratched and stained, though the original finish can be restored without difficulty. Marble will require resealing once or twice a year to maintain its protective finish.

②

①

③

① To re-create a period look, off-white marble with misty veining is the ideal complement to chrome.

② The sophistication of this gray marble vanity top, with backsplash and central sink, is complemented by a brushed-steel faucet.

③ This vanity features a simple curved white basin recessed into a light oak cabinet with a black slate top, creating an uncomplicated but stylish look.

④ Natural oak units enrich the tone of this kitchen, while the black granite island unit and countertops add contrast; a gray marble tabletop introduces color and texture.

⑤ Pale pink marble countertops flank the walls of this minimalist kitchen, while green glass backsplashes add cool freshness.

⑥ Marble can be polished to a highly mirrored finish. Even the black of this countertop reflects the kitchen's wood tones.

⑦ Granite can be carved to accommodate sink recesses of various shapes and even to allow drainage, as shown here.

⑥

④

⑤

⑦

Countertops and vanities
are available in an immense variety of stone colors, usually in granite, basalt, slate, and quartz. Less durable but wonderfully attractive are marble, travertine, limestone, and soapstone. Select color and pattern according to your theme. Dark, plain stones are sophisticated and stylish in contemporary décor, as they call for more subdued complementary colors. Enliven them with chrome fittings, stainless steel, and glass. Stones in more earthy browns, reds, and beiges tend to complement more traditional settings and furnishings.

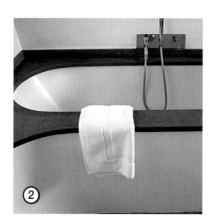

① Brown polished granite vanity top
② Gray slate bath surround
③ Beige granite vanity top
④ Natural oatmeal travertine, unfilled
⑤ Pink, black, and gray granite vanity top
⑥ Gray granite vanity top
⑦ White marble bath surround
⑧ Black and brown granite countertop
⑨ Black granite countertop
⑩ Gold and black marble countertop
⑪ Black slate countertop with honed finish
⑫ Gold and gray marble countertop
⑬ Black honed basalt countertop
⑭ Cream limestone countertop
⑮ Multicolored marble countertop
⑯ Black basalt countertop with double-thickness edge
⑰ Black basalt with sink recesses
⑱ Cream limestone countertop with twin sinks and drainer slots
⑲ White limestone countertop
⑳ Black and gray granite countertop

⑨

⑬

⑰

⑩

⑭

⑱

⑪

⑮

⑲

⑫

⑯

⑳

Basins, Baths, and Showers

Today's fashion in sanitaryware is to renounce the mass-produced, plain, and monotonous vitreous china and plastic basins, baths, bidets, shower trays, and toilets of yesteryear and opt for fittings with a more craftsmanlike quality. Stone sanitaryware ranges from delicate, individual washbowls hewn from marble, travertine, and limestone—which are simply perched on a shelf—to shallow, square trays of slate, and floorstanding pedestals that defy comparison with any other kitchen or bathroom essentials. A bathtub carved from solid stone is surely the ultimate in bathroom luxury, resembling either a chunky tub chiseled from a solid block of rock, or a slender, curved shell lovingly pared away to smoothness. Stone surfaces used in the kitchen and bathroom must be sealed to protect them from stains and to make cleaning easier. Wax or silicone sealers are generally used. Porous stones need more frequent sealing than granite or marble.

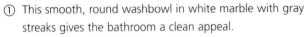

① This smooth, round washbowl in white marble with gray streaks gives the bathroom a clean appeal.

② This slimline gray slate shower floor has a series of grooves cut in its surface for a safe, nonslip finish.

③ Solid and sturdy, a stone bathtub such as this would demand a suitably strong and rigid floor to support it.

④ Lustrous marble is used throughout this bathroom—even the tub and washbowl are carved from milky-white stone—creating an opulent finish.

⑤ This ramp-style basin in beige limestone features a backward-sloping tray that discharges water through the broad slot located at the back of the basin.

⑥ A honed black granite vanity unit mounted on sturdy granite pedestals has a front fascia to give the impression that it is actually a solid slab.

Basins, baths, and showers in natural stone or cast varieties range in color from pale yellows and pinks to earthy reds, honed grays, or bespeckled, veined marbles in multitudes of tones, some with a gorgeous translucency. Interior finishes are, of course, perfectly smooth for comfort, hygiene, and impermeability. Outer faces may be smooth or textured with thousands of tiny pits (roughly carved or riven). Most fittings, faucets, and other paraphernalia are starkly modern, either separate or freestanding. This contrast accentuates the refreshing originality that has entirely changed the concept of how we see and use the bathroom and kitchen.

① Oval-molded stone resin tub, speckled cream limestone
② Square-molded stone resin tub, speckled cream limestone
③ Honed, carved limestone tub
④ Carved travertine tub
⑤ Carved white marble sink and niches
⑥ Beige limestone shower floor
⑦ Carved natural stone pedestal sink
⑧ Black basalt shower tray with inset grid
⑨ Honed black basalt round basin
⑩ Honed black basalt round washbowl
⑪ Round travertine washbowl with a honed interior and chiseled exterior
⑫ Rectangular honed white limestone basin
⑬ Rectangular honed gray marble basin
⑭ Honed black basalt vanity unit
⑮ Cream carved limestone vanity unit
⑯ Individual carved stone washbowls

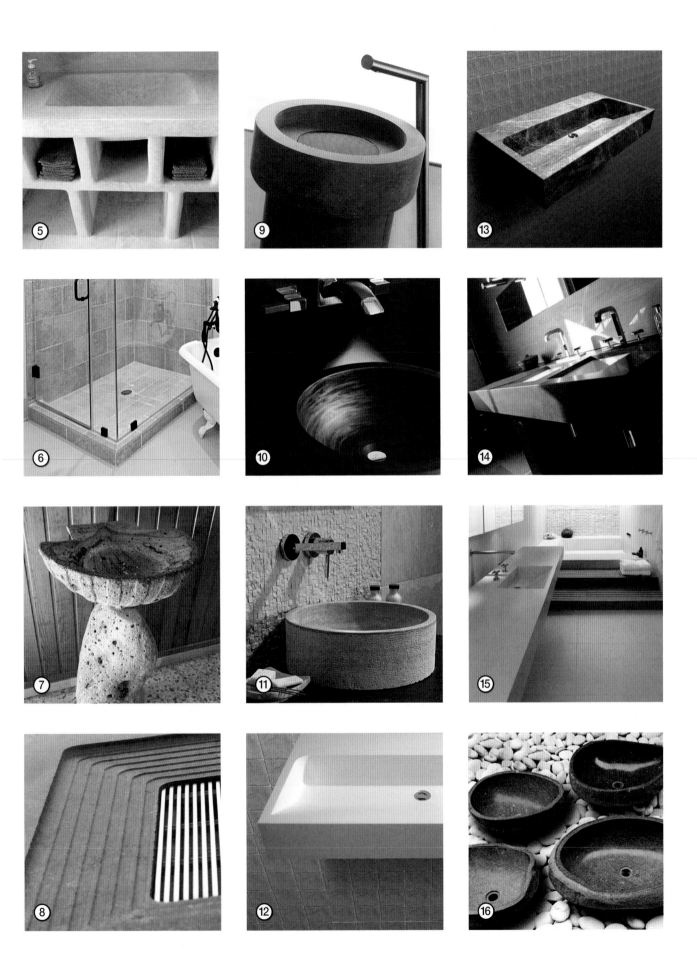

Fire Surrounds

The sight of flames flickering in the hearth is mesmerizing. Central heating, however, largely rendered the open fire redundant. With the removal of the fireplace, many rooms lost their essential focal point. However, people are increasingly turning back to the open fire—or the wood- or coal-burning stove—as a means of secondary heating, and as a feature that restores a room's balance and direction. Fire surrounds usually comprise separate side columns, or pilasters, with a mantel above a frieze. Some types have a decorative tiled or metal insert, or inlays of stone. Hearths are generally separate slabs or a cladding of stone tiles. There are many custom-made surround styles employed by designers.

① Choose a marble fire surround in a period style to add a picturesque element to a bedroom. Enhance the look with ornaments and flowers.

② Sandstone blocks are soft enough to be carved into beautiful curves, as shown in the side columns of this massive open fireplace.

③ A tall, white limestone surround with a large mantel frames this fire opening, creating a purely decorative focal point.

④ Modern woodburners use metal flues to extract smoke, and can be installed where no chimney exists. This corner fireplace is clad with sandstone blocks concealing the metal flue.

⑤ Many chimneys were removed from older properties during modernization, but they can be reinstated with period style replacements such as this baroque surround and tall chimney piece made from cast stone.

⑥ Gray and white marble tiles with swirling patterns that resemble smoke clad this chimney piece, curved side columns, and raised hearth, creating a very modern design for this open fireplace.

3

5

4

6

Fire surrounds in stone can often be restored. If the original has been removed, an original salvaged from another house can be installed or a modern replica of a traditional style—in natural stone or cast stone—can be fitted. New surrounds are also made in a range of traditional and modern styles, from highly ornate to understated.

① Carved limestone: half-round molding, slab hearth
② Carved limestone: fluted pilasters, rosette capitals, slab hearth
③ Carved marble: fluted pilasters, Ionic capitals, frieze with a central tablet, framing an inlay of green marble
④ Carved marble: pilasters, frieze, capitals decorated with foliage garlands
⑤ Carved marble: French corbels, break-fronted mantel, black marble inlays
⑥ Carved white limestone: Victorian style
⑦ Carved white marble: Louis XV style
⑧ Carved white marble: Georgian style; black marble columns and inlays
⑨ Carved white marble
⑩ Carved white marble: Queen Anne style
⑪ Carved white marble: Adams style; Ionic columns, urn, drapery frieze
⑫ Carved white marble: George III style; Sienna marble columns, frieze flutes
⑬ Carved sandstone: Tudor Gothic style
⑭ Sandstone curved cornerpiece: coursed slabs and blocks, marble hearth
⑮ Cast limestone: Gothic arch and moldings, slab hearth
⑯ Cast limestone: Tudor style; coursed back blocks and hearth
⑰ Honed Portland stone chimney piece: hearth, matching fire bowl
⑱ Contemporary surround for gas fireplace, LED illuminated
⑲ Contemporary surround: writhing flamelike strands
⑳ Carved Portland stone and black fossil limestone: Rococo style

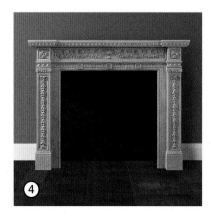

9

13

17

10

14

18

11

15

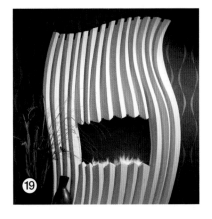
19

12

16

20

Staircases and Balustrades

A stone stairway makes a luxurious, sophisticated statement in a hallway, where it forms the focal point of an ostentatious display. Stone stairways may be constructed entirely of stone or of reinforced concrete clad with stone slabs for the treads or the risers or both. Treads and risers may be supported within the walls of the stairwell or on supports called "stringboards" at one or both sides, which may also be stone. Some open-tread flights have a metal frame, with stone slabs used for the treads; and no risers. Cantilevered and elliptical stone stairs are some of the most elegant and graceful, and appear to defy gravity. Stone balustrades consist of a shaped handrail and base channel, with shapely "turned" balusters, or straight rails in stone. The ends of the handrail and base channel are attached to sturdy stone newel posts at the top and bottom of the flight, or at intermediate landings where a flight changes direction.

①

① Elliptical staircases are elegant. This flight is made from Portland stone (a mellow limestone from Dorset, Great Britain). The black metal balustrade with gold embellishment complements the fine lines of the staircase.

② Honed beige limestone slabs form the treads and risers of this modern flight, while an unusual glass balustrade creates a feeling of space and light.

③ Worn by the passage of many feet, this natural stone stairway has a sturdy stone balustrade painted pure white for contrast.

④ This spiral staircase—which makes enchanting use of natural light—has been embellished with wooden treads.

⑤ Marble, with an added carpet runner and stair rods, is the perfect partner for this elegant iron balustrade. Marble heightens luxury wherever it is used.

②

4

5

Stone stairways in all styles—straight stairs, curving spirals, and straight flights with intermediate landings (and half-landings)—are all available from specialist installers, in a range of stone varieties. Popular varieties of stone include granite, marble, and slate. Treads must, of course, be slip-free, so honed or flamed finishes are generally provided. Treads with polished surfaces incorporate a slip-prevention strip or cut grooves. If you consider a stone balustrade to be too bulky, stone stairways can alternatively be complemented with wooden or metal balustrades for a more elegant look.

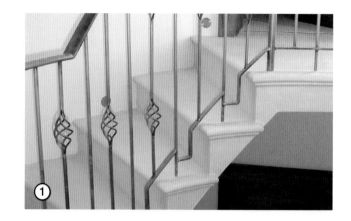

① Flamed limestone staircase with metal balustrade and handrail
② Ancient worn stone granite spiral
③ Golden marble flight with red veining
④ Pinkish white marble flight with metal balustrade
⑤ Polished brown marble with black and gray veining
⑥ Polished Jerusalem stone treads and risers with wall string
⑦ White marble treads and risers with red and white marble stringboards
⑧ Spiral in sandstone, with supporting column, winding stone handrail, and turned balusters
⑨ Gray polished marble flight with anti-slip grooves, stone balustrade
⑩ Greenish gray honed fossil limestone steps and balustrade
⑪ Sandstone flight with bullnose treads
⑫ Limestone stringboards supporting slab treads and risers, glass balustrade

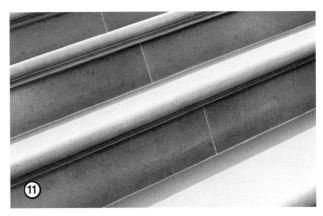

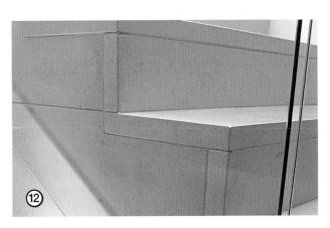

Exterior Stone Paving

Real stone paving not only looks great, but it also provides the practical, durable hard surfaces you need for exterior landscaping. Commonly paved areas include paths and steps for safe and convenient access through the garden, driveways for automobiles, and patios for relaxing and enjoying the outdoors. There's a wealth of paving slabs, smaller stone tiles, square stone setts, rounded cobblestones, and even gravel available to create texture, pattern, and color.

Without stone paving we'd all be trudging through acres of mud surrounding our homes. Although you can obtain stone types from different regions—even different countries—you should take into account whether the appearance of an exotic material would visibly jar with materials that proliferate locally, or with the style of your house.

When designing a path, remember to measure the width according to its anticipated usage. A narrow path of about 30 inches (76 cm) wide, for example, might be sufficient for access for one person with a wheelbarrow, but a path of this width wouldn't allow two people to stroll side by side. An entry path, therefore, should be about 4 feet (1.2 m) wide.

Consider a patio's location, taking into account where the sun rises and sets, how much natural shade is provided by trees or shrubs, and what the view is like. Will you be gazing at a splendid panorama or looking directly into your neighbor's backyard? The size of your patio depends largely on the space you have available, but the best guide is the furniture that you intend to use. Taking into account

any planting areas you want to include within the paving, position the furniture where you want it and allow for a minimum margin of 16 inches (40 cm) beyond it, erring on the generous side where possible.

Paved surfaces need adequate foundations in order to avoid sinking, becoming dangerously uneven, or cracking due to seasonal expansion and contraction of the ground. For a path, in areas not affected by freezing conditions, lay a base of 4 inches (10 cm) of deep gravel; where freezing is likely, double the depth of the base. Level off with 1 to 2 inches (2.5–5 cm) of sand and install the paving on top. For a patio, you'll need a deeper base of well-compacted gravel and sand. Check your local codes and regulations for specific instructions. For soft ground you'll need substantial foundations— perhaps even poured concrete.

Paving abutting a house requires specific grading and preparation work to avoid rainwater splashing the wall above or seeping into the foundations. Again, before you begin to install your paving check with your local land regulation office for suggestions and laws specific to your region.

Opposite: Irregular-shaped sandstone slabs laid in a random pattern form a distinctive entry path to this modern home, highlighting the color of the stone walls and emphasizing the angularity of the façade.

Below: A broad, glazed arch opens on to a charming patio, itself decked in soft gray slabs.

Types, Sizes, and Finishes

Limestone, sandstone, quartzite, granite, and slate are widely available for exterior paving. With bold, riven faces or smooth—but nevertheless nonslip—tumbled antique or honed finishes, many colors are available: white, cream, yellow, brown, rust, blue, green, gray, and black. Slabs range in size from a modest 4 x 4 inches to a massive 48 x 48 inches (10 x 10 cm to 120 x 120 cm), rising in approximately 4-inch (10-cm) increments. Rectangular units within a similar size range are also available. Many suppliers can even provide larger and nonstandard sizes to order, and some sell "patio packs" containing a range of shapes, sizes, and colors to re-create a specific design. Slabs suitable for exterior use are about 1 or 2 inches (3 or 5 cm) thick, though some thinner types can be adhered outside to a cast concrete substrate. Slab edges are either straight sawn or riven—straight cuts allow slabs to be aligned accurately with narrow joint lines for a more formal effect, while rough-edged slabs are more suitable for a less formal layout. Special shapes include circular and segmented hexagons and octagons.

① Mix up shapes and sizes to lessen formality. Huge granite slabs bring nature into this outdoor kitchen.

② Large square marble slabs are laid diagonally on the floor of this grand exterior dining room.

③ Gray gravel is used as ground cover surrounding this modern water feature, with minimal planting for impact.

④ Geometric paving can be encased in a concrete border, as it has been on this dining patio. Here the color contrast due to the stained concrete adds emphasis.

⑤ A substantial dividing wall is mirrored by a half wall to create a dramatic entry path to this home. The colors were all chosen carefully to blend with house and path.

①

Slate Paving

Slate's fine-grained texture and distinctive blues, blue-grays, greens, and purples make it a popular material for exterior paving. It's an exceptionally versatile stone, with random-shaped riven paving being an excellent choice for the cottage garden patio and more regular shapes such as checkerboard designs with mixed colors suited to modern patios. Tumbled slate paving has a distressed, aged look, with crumbled edges and corners. Old, broken roofing slates can also be laid on edge, with most of the strips buried, to create a decorative border or edging (this is helpful in allowing a mower to cut right up to the edge of an estate). Similar stones to slate, which are worth looking out for and which may be cheaper options, include the blue-gray to turquoise whinstone from Scotland and the northeast of England, the highly durable and intensely colored quartzite, and the extremely nonslip porphyry, a favorite for poolside paving.

① An elaborate swimming pool is paved with gold-mottled slate in an offset grid. Contrast is created by random pieces used within distinctive edging.

② Slate, even when wet, is highly nonslip—the ideal choice for exterior paving, particularly when regularly doused with water, as with this slate-tile-clad raised water feature, designed to overflow with water at a regular rate.

③ Mellowed by the rock garden encroaching on its perimeter, this rustic patio features several sizes of gray and gold slate in an abstract pattern.

④ Blue-gray slate squares bordered by random slate slabs in warm metallic hues reflect the colors of sky and earth.

⑤ Narrow strips of metallic-colored slate are laid in staggered rows, forming a grid for the arrangement of the abstract steel plant holders that comprise the centerpiece of this modern patio.

⑥ A subtle blend of the natural tones of wood and stone is achieved with this immensely hardwearing porphyry paving.

2

3

5

4

6

Slate was at one time only available in the areas surrounding its sources—such as Wales and Cornwall in Britain, where notable varieties originate. However, slate is now imported from countries such as Brazil, India, and China (China supplies most of this market). Take care when buying imported slate, since it might not be suitable for outdoor use in wet climates; poor quality slate is likely to delaminate in such conditions. The metallic, multicolored luster of Chinese Peacock Slate, for example, tends to fade with regular wear, and sealing and regular cleaning are necessary. Porphyry, a type of volcanic stone, is mined in China, Argentina, Pakistan, and Italy, and exported to North America and Europe, while major sources of quartzite include India and China.

① Gold and gray slate slabs
② Gray slate with gold insets and sawn borders
③ Slate shards and beachstones within slate-on-edge framing
④ Mossy slate
⑤ Red slate in a running bond
⑥ Brown and gray slate in a random pattern
⑦ Green, purple, and gray slate in a random pattern, jointed
⑧ Random black slate with white pointing
⑨ Sawn, honed black slate
⑩ Sawn, honed gray slate
⑪ Sawn, honed tan porphyry with recessed joints
⑫ Multicolor quartzite with colored pointing

Limestone Paving

Limestone was crushed by the Romans and used as a base for their roads, and was then popular during the 18th and 19th centuries as a building stone. Limestone is also a base material for making lime, cement, and mortar. Although susceptible to the long term effects of acid rain—which stains and dissolves it—limestone is a popular alternative to sandstone paving because of its hardwearing properties and its fine surface texture. Easy to work, it can be cut and shaped with saws and hand tools. Limestone can be supplied either with a riven finish or it can be honed, which is ideal when a level surface such as an outdoor dining area is necessary.

① Smart, polished limestone with watery graining has a touch of formality that is well suited to this stylish and modern setting.

② This radiant pinkish yellow limestone reflects the rich colors of its origin in the south of France.

③ Beige fossil limestone slabs have been cut on a gradual crescent shape to surround the perimeter of this tranquil pond.

④ Limestone paving can be used as the decking for a roof terrace provided the structure is sound and can support the weight of the slabs.

⑤ The glasslike surface of this swimming pool is enhanced by subtle paving in ultra-flat, honed limestone.

⑥ Enormous honey limestone slabs with broad, gold joints tone to perfection with the woven reed furniture and sun-gold upholstery shown here.

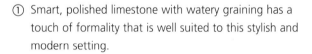

Limestone is a sedimentary rock primarily containing calcium carbonate, which, in its purest form, is white. However, because of mineral inclusions, limestone paving comes in a range of colors—from yellow, red, and blue to steely gray and black. Subtle colors and minimal variation make limestone suitable for both modern and traditional settings. Jerusalem stone is predominantly golden in color, but it is also found in off-white and subtle gray tones.

Jerusalem stone, sourced in Israel, has been regarded as exotic and unique since biblical times. A natural dolomite-limestone, it displays a depth of golden color greater than other limestone. It is richly evocative of its country of origin, where it is a widely used building material.

① French honey-colored limestone, sawn edges
② Black honed limestone, white pointing
③ Cream limestone, sawn edges
④ Jerusalem stone
⑤ Gray mottled limestone, wide mortar joints
⑥ Pink-toned mottled limestone, wide mortar joints
⑦ Blue-gray riven limestone, colored joints
⑧ Green and brown mottled limestone, colored joints
⑨ Jerusalem stone, sawn edges
⑩ Buff, white, and cream riven limestone
⑪ Gray-blue sawn limestone with bullnose edging
⑫ Chiseled gray limestone with honed bullnose edging

Granite Paving

Granite is one of the most hardwearing stones, and is endowed with a glistening sparkle that catches the sunlight and gives it an air of distinction—or sometimes even a glamorous look. The surface of this durable stone can be worked in numerous ways: honed to a soft, nonslip sheen; polished to a high gloss (best reserved for outdoor feature areas); pounded with a spiked metal hammer or chiseled to give it a rough texture; machine-sawn for straight, regular edges; split for a rugged, riven edge; or sandblasted to expose its granulations. Tumbled stones are artificially aged, with crumbled edges and corners and a distressed surface finish. Flamed granite becomes even more hardwearing, with a slip-resistant finish. Eminently suitable for outdoor use, granite is highly frost-resistant and naturally impervious, yet weathers and wears attractively.

① Granite's natural imperviousness makes it an ideal candidate for an informal stepping-stone bridge across a stream or pond.

② This colorful terrace is styled as a clearing within a forest. The surface of random granite slabs are softened by dainty terra-cotta pots and delicate furniture.

③ This path of irregular-shaped granite slabs winding through a lush garden is positioned to create an air of mystery.

④ Break up a broad, straight flight of granite steps by insetting a large boulder and planting low-growing alpines in the cracks and crevices to soften the effect.

⑤ Tough, durable, and smart, gray granite is used here to create a formal flight of steps in which each rectangular slab forms the tread and riser of the flight.

⑥ Gray, bespeckled granite and black granite are teamed up here to create a glamorous poolside scheme.

⑦ Cool, gray granite with a light-catching gleam offsets glizty black and orange styling on this movie-set terrace.

(6)

(4)

(5)

(7)

Granite comes in an enormous range of colors and shades: white, light and dark gray, yellow, red, green, blue, and black. Each base color is likely to be infused with glistening, granular speckles and with an overall mottled effect in contrasting hues. Depending on its surface treatment, granite is equally at home in a rustic garden or a traditional setting, and can also be transformed into a thoroughly modern material for contemporary garden styles.

① Pale, flamed, various sizes
② Gray, random shape, filled joints
③ Pink, random shape, sawn
④ Pink and red, random shape, fractured edge
⑤ Gray setts, radius pattern
⑥ Gray, red, and black in a geometric grid
⑦ Multicolor setts, weathered finish
⑧ Gray, random shape, broken
⑨ Pale gray, sawn
⑩ Brown and white tumbled setts
⑪ Silver-gray and black, sawn
⑫ Yellow, with red and blue inclusions

1

Sandstone Paving

Sandstone is a sedimentary rock formed by sand-sized grains cementing together. The youngest of the quartz-based stones (which would eventually become quartzite if subjected to heat and pressure), it has a fine, granular finish and uniform texture. Paving materials are available with various surface textures. The undulating cleft texture is achieved by splitting the stone along its edge; flamed sandstone has a rough finish produced by heating the stone, which bursts the crystals within; polished sandstone is characterized by enhanced coloring (but is slippery and best reserved for feature areas); honed stone has a smooth, soft, and nonslip sheen (but is more porous than natural stone); hammered stone has a pitted and grooved surface; sawn stone has a semi-smooth, coarsely polished, but regular finish; and sandblasting gives a matte finish similar to the cleft finish.

① Shades of golden, white, and gray random-shaped sandstone paving create the varying tones and textures of earth, which helps to blend this natural style swimming pool with its rocky surroundings.

② Soft and mellow sandstone paving provides a neutral background, enhancing the coloring of flowers and foliage, and blending well with the burnt earth brickwork of this raised planting bed.

③ Alternating squares and rectangles of gold, mint green, and pink sandstone together form a broad, richly textured entry path.

④ Sawn slabs in two tones of buff-colored sandstone display distinctive streaks that strongly resemble the grain of oak.

⑤ Use different colored paving to create patterns. The honed black slate slabs used here form bold contrasting squares within an area of riven sandstone tinged with green and pink, emphasizing the shape of the patio.

⑥ Random-shaped slabs of sandstone in four different tones create the distinctive design of a tortoise shell.

Sandstone color depends on the mineral contents and impurities in the sand, but generally ranges from white, yellow, red, beige, pink, brown, green, and gray to an array of other rainbow colors. Sandstone is found in many parts of the world, with notable types including the red sandstones from the southwest and west of England and Wales, central Europe, and Mongolia, and the reddish tints to dark terracotta colors of the southwestern United States. The northern English county of Yorkshire yields the durable, tight-grained Yorkstone popular for paving. Much of today's sandstone is exported from India, and is often considerably more affordable than local types.

① Random Yorkstone
② Riven beige
③ Riven black and gray
④ Riven fossil, coral
⑤ Honed fossil, pink
⑥ Honed gray sawn strips
⑦ Honed gray slabs with streaks
⑧ Riven gray
⑨ Honed multicolor
⑩ Riven brown and red, polished
⑪ Riven purple
⑫ Sandblasted lemon with pink streaks

Gravel, Cobblestones, and Setts

Setts, also known as "cubes," are sawn or split-faced, rustic pavers that can be used as borders or patterns to soften the regularity of larger scale paving slabs. They are also suitable for surfacing driveways and hardstandings. Although firm, a flat base is essential to prevent the pavers from sinking and the surface becoming too uneven. Pavers range in size from about 4 x 4 inches (10 x 10 cm) to 8 x 10 inches (20 x 25 cm), with a thickness of 6 to 8 inches (15–20 cm). True cubes measuring 4 x 4 x 4 inches (10 x 10 x 10 cm) and 5 x 5 x 5 inches (12.5 x 12.5 x 12.5 cm) are the most popular. Setts are sometimes incorrectly described as cobbles.

Cobbles, or cobblestones, originate in riverbeds and beaches. They are rounded, irregular, undressed stones measuring between about 3 inches (7.5 cm) to 10 inches (25.5 cm). Unlike flat-topped setts, cobbles are not comfortable stones to walk on, and are sometimes reserved for feature areas or areas where you want to discourage walking.

Gravel can be used as a surface dressing for a path or driveway. It is composed of small rounded or angular stones, about ½ to 1 inch (6–30 mm) in diameter. Angular types are a byproduct of quarry blasting, while round types are from fluvial sources such as riverbeds. Washed gravel is cleaned to remove fine dust. Self-binding gravel retains the dust to produce a surface that becomes loosely bound and resistant to redistribution from foot traffic, though not permanently solid like concrete.

① Fine gravel, retained by terra-cotta rope edging, does not detract from the elegance of this entrance. A classical planter and box hedge set the tone.

② Gravel is the ideal medium for filling in awkward areas where other large-scale paving material would be difficult to use.

③ Tumbled gray basalt setts create the appearance of breadth in this path that opens out into a driveway.

④ Leave gaps between pavers to let grasses grow through. The divison between garden and patio will be blurred, as demonstrated in this romantic breakfast corner.

⑤ Circular bands of cream limestone setts combine with radius-cut black slate to create a dramatic patio design.

⑥ Granite setts make a gentle transition with a sunbleached wood deck, while stepping stones bedded in gravel add further subtle texture.

Gravel, cobblestones, and setts offer tremendous design possibilities, whether you want to create the charm of a traditional cobbled street, the elegance of an old-style courtyard, or the classic country style of a gravel path or driveway. Setts and cobbles can be used to create swirling patterns such as fans, spirals, and circles. They can also be laid in even courses, like brickwork, with staggered joints in each row, or in a random fashion. Setts are produced in both the harder igneous and softer sedimentary stone types. The smaller stones are frequently granite or basalt. They come in sawn, honed, or hammered finishes and in colors ranging from white and yellow to red, blue, black and many speckled varieties.

Gravel used for surface dressing paths should be about ¼- to ⅜-inch (6–10 mm). For driveways, use ⅜- to ¾-inch (10–18 mm). Gravel must be laid on firm foundations of crushed and compacted stone or rubble, about 4 inches (10 cm) deep for a path and 6 inches (15 cm) for a driveway. Check with local authorities for exact measurements for your region. Borders, such as brick, stone, wood, or concrete, are recommended to prevent the gravel from spreading and mixing with the surrounding soil. Gravel can also be raked for a Japanese-garden effect, or used to cover soil in a Mediterranean-style garden.

① Multicolored "pea" gravel
② Predominantly beige gravel
③ Red granite setts, random bond, black gravel pointing
④ Tumbled gray granite setts, cube and radius
⑤ Light and dark gray setts, tumbled
⑥ Sawn blue and red setts, mottled yellow
⑦ White angular gravel
⑧ Brown sandstone setts and large, rounded gravel
⑨ Mixed brown sawn sandstone setts, running bond
   with inset circle
⑩ Mixed granite setts, tumbled (left) and sawn (right)
⑪ Pink setts, running bond
⑫ Yellow granite cobbles, rounded faces

Shapes and Sizes

There are thousands of possible paving patterns. Slabs are available in a wide range of shapes, including squares, rectangles, octagons, and others. Your design may be nothing more than a simple checkerboard, a staggered running bond, or a zigzag herringbone or as complex as random or repeating patterns of different sizes, materials, and colors.

The most basic pattern for square or rectangular slabs is the checkerboard design, based on a rigid grid with the paving butted edge to edge. The effect is practical and effective, but visually static. Simply staggering the joints by up to half the slab's length will break up the grid effect and introduce a "direction" to the scheme, rather like the effect used on sidewalks. This can be used to visually increase the length of the paving area.

Alternatively, you can make the checkerboard pattern look less utilitarian by introducing rows of small-scale stone setts or even bricks between the slabs in width and length. This type of elegant pattern not only looks attractive but will also cost about half that of more complex designs.

Further break up a uniform grid by combining square and rectangular tiles, or create a more random pattern by mixing several shapes and sizes of slab, laid in a jigsaw fashion. Although the effect is visually "random," the layout does need to be planned in detail. There are some basic rules you should follow with this type of pattern: four corners of slab should never meet and no joint should run for more than about 10 feet (3 m), since this would destroy the randomness of the overall pattern.

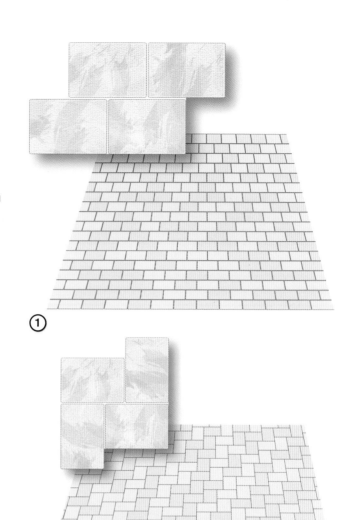

① Running bond
② Herringbone
③ Running bond, offset
④ Random layout rules
⑤ Random repeating A
⑥ Random repeating B
⑦ Random repeating C
⑧ Random repeating D

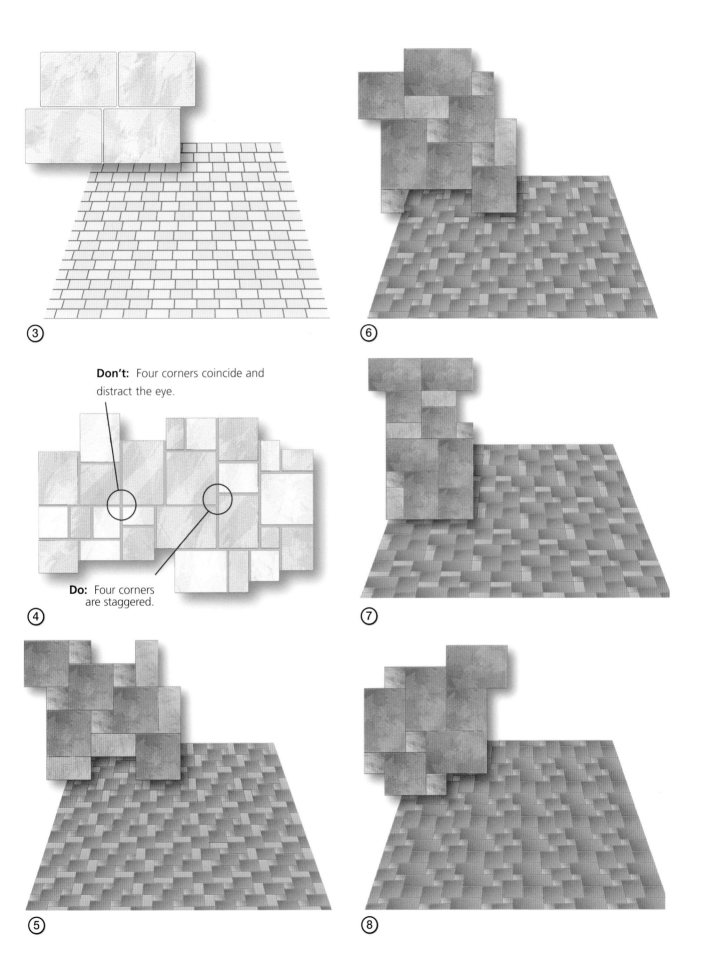

③

Don't: Four corners coincide and distract the eye.

Do: Four corners are staggered.

④

⑤

⑥

⑦

⑧

Colors and Textures

While the size and shape of paving
slabs can be used to create formal or
random patterns, color and texture
can be used to accentuate the
design. Simply adapting the plain
checkerboard pattern by alternating,
for example, cream- and red-colored
slabs will enliven an otherwise plain,
utilitarian scheme. Contrast textures
for visual interest: for example,
alternate riven-faced gray slate slabs
with smooth-faced sandstone to
create a pleasing mixture of textures
and colors. Avoid too great a mixture
of colors and textures or the effect
will be disjointed on the eye. When
embellishing a basic grid format with
rows of small-scale paving, such as
setts, use a color and texture that
contrasts with the overall surface.

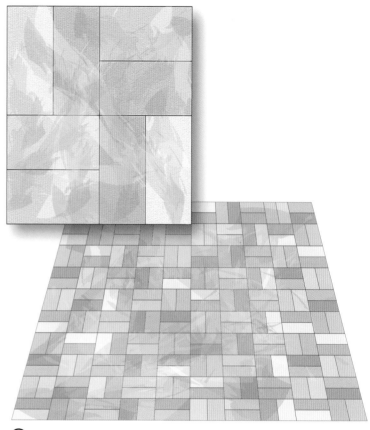

① Basket weave of mixed color
② Block pattern
③ Barred square
④ Sandstone with gravel
⑤ Checkerboard A
⑥ Checkerboard B

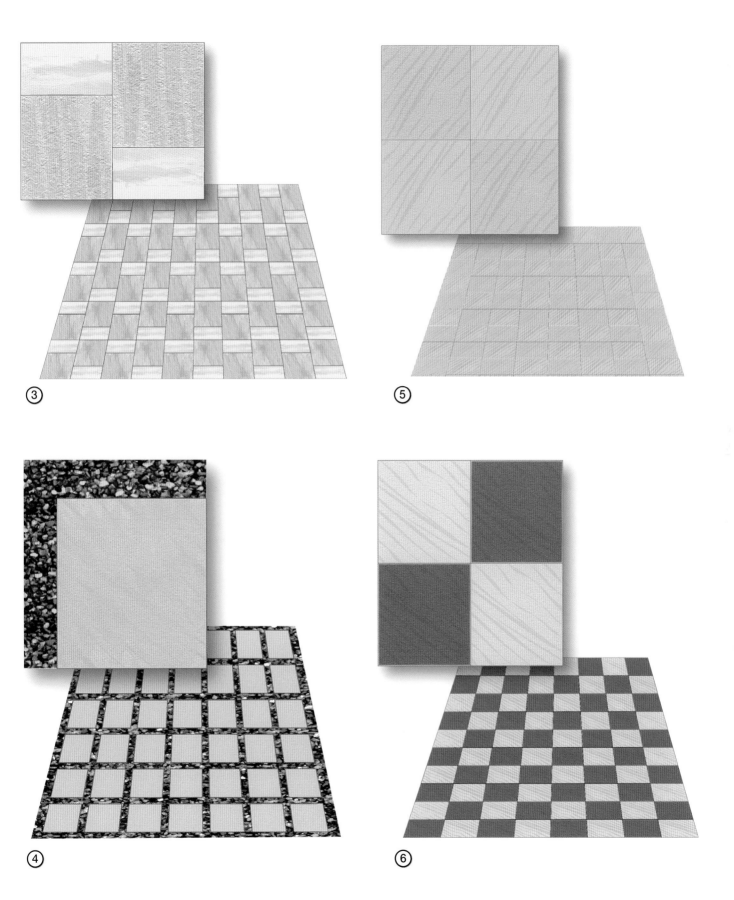

③

⑤

④

⑥

Patterns

Given the sizes of the slabs you intend to use, it's best to plan your patterns on paper (or a computer CAD program) first—this is much less laborious than hefting the actual slabs into place onsite. Most suppliers will provide suggested layouts suitable for the range of slabs they stock, and some sell the paving in batches of mixed sizes sufficient to create a module of the pattern. This makes it easy to estimate the number of modules you will need to cover the area of your paving.

For a more formal but highly decorative pattern you can lay rectangular slabs in a zigzag herringbone, basketweave, or parquet design. Alternatively, create a basic pattern from a square slab—or a square of setts—framed by rectangular slabs. Repeat this across the area to be paved, perhaps separating each "frame" with rows of setts.

Slabs can also be laid in curves and circles using radius-cut units (ideal for creating a meandering pathway or introducing curved patterns in an overall geometric design). The small-scale granite setts are ideal for installing complex fantail bonds, multiple-row circular patterns, or curving parallel rows that follow the winding profile of a pathway.

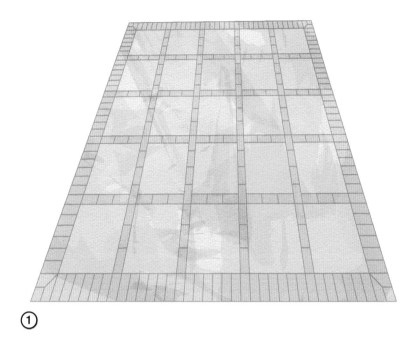

①

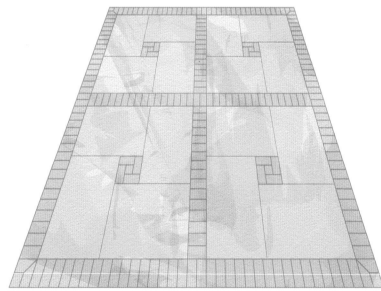

②

① Checkerboard with pavers
② Squares framed with pavers
③ Common driveway pattern
④ Random setts
⑤ Radial pattern
⑥ Fan pattern

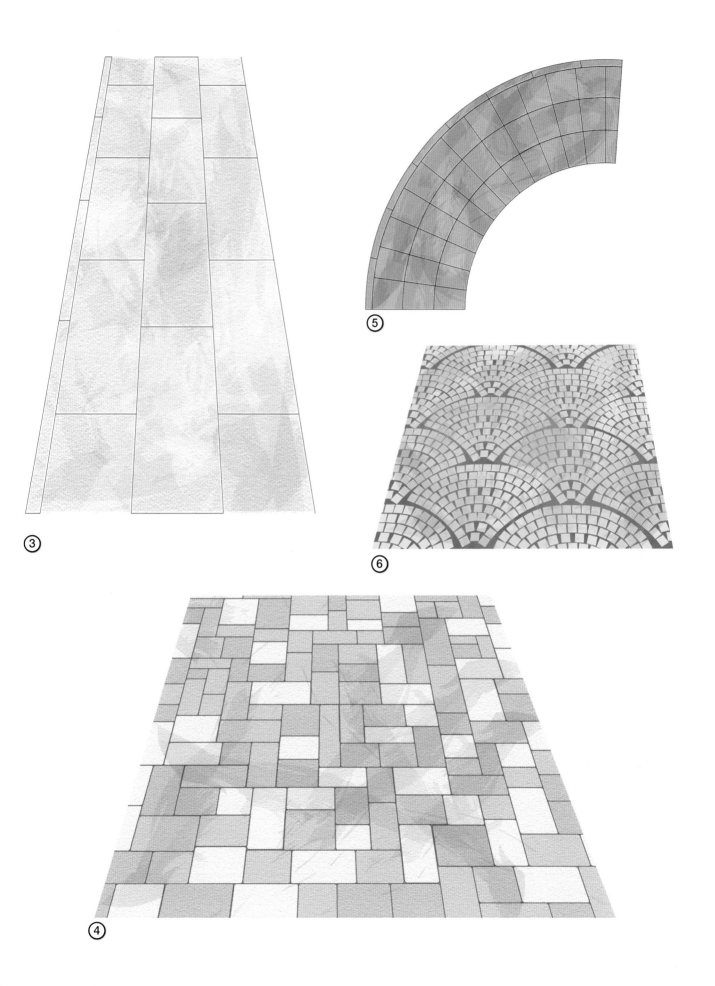

③

⑤

⑥

④

Landscaping Stone

Landscaping stone includes both natural stone, used largely for its attractive appearance, and stone blocks, used to create highly functional yet aesthetically pleasing structures such as walls and steps. Stonework forms the building blocks of your garden plan. You can introduce land variances in an otherwise plain, flat plot by constructing earth-retaining walls, creating terraces, and building flights of steps to link the various parts of your garden. Introduce areas of interest in a small or otherwise featureless backyard by dividing up the area with stone walls.

Rock has presence and character. It's hard to ignore, and for that reason it needs to be treated with a sensitive eye and used in moderation—unless your aim is to create a garden that resembles a barren mountainside. This is not to say that there isn't a place for gardens based on hard materials, with only limited space devoted to plant life, but the plantings in these cases need to be well chosen. We're not all horticulturalists, and a rock garden can often appear out of keeping with colorful borders of swaying perennials and pretty annuals. Attempts at combining two themes within one yard frequently result in uneasy marriages; between the highlands and the lowlands, for example, or the urban and the rural.

The overall shape and style of your garden is determined by the structures it contains. This may be nothing more than a stone wall marking the boundary between your property and the street or your neighbor's property. The style of wall you choose should complement that of the house itself, and the materials used to build it should inspire a sense of unity. The wall may be high—within permitted rules—to ensure privacy and security, or low and topped with a wooden fence or metal railing.

Within your property, build walls to contain specific areas. This works well to limit access to a single doorway or gate and also to safely enclose swimming pools or fishponds. Alternatively, delineate a formal lawn with low surrounding walls. A high visual barrier adds privacy to your yard or garden. A dividing wall also provides a support for climbing plants and wind protection for vulnerable specimens in any adjoining beds.

An entrance within a wall can be used for a wooden or metal gate or a door and may incorporate a stone arch. Long walls require intermediate pilasters to add strength, and these can be topped with finials, statues, urns, or lamps (for night-time appreciation of the garden). Walls need not be totally solid—a circular hole within a wall adds interest and provides a tantalizing glimpse of the area beyond.

A low wall around a paved patio, if it is filled with wide coping, can double as seating or as a plinth for holding potted plants and urns. If it is hollow, a low wall can be filled with soil and planted. You could even incorporate a grill and use the space in between walls as an area for cookouts.

Raised planting beds and hollow walls filled with soil are both great options for wheelchair users, since all the necessary plant care can be carried out from a comfortable seated position.

Above: Create the impression of an ancient rustic garden wall with blocks of rough-hewn sandstone in rich gold. Allow glossy green ivy to clamber over the surface to soften the effect. Keep the ivy trimmed back to prevent its tendrils from infiltrating the mortar joints.

Opposite: Strong in shape and form, broad sandstone steps rise between dry walls of thick and thin slabs. A large boulder is added to evoke a natural feel.

1

Natural Stone

Use natural stone in the garden both for its aesthetic value and to enhance your planting designs. Natural stone boulders straight from the quarry can be used to create powerful landscape features such as rock gardens, waterfalls, or specific areas of interest. Stone can also radically transform the appearance of a plain garden by introducing rugged shape and form, or bolster what is already there with texture and color.

An entirely rock-based garden, with exposed boulders surrounded by beds of shale and gravel, can be just as visually stimulating as a floral garden. Areas of conventional garden with lawns and flowerbeds can also be transformed with artfully placed natural rocks. The secret of a successful, natural-looking rock garden is to use stones that resemble true rocky outcrops, rather than rounded boulders piled in a heap on flat ground. In the natural world, erosion causes

subtle exposure of stone. Also, uncovered rock tends to appear to lean at an angle in the earth rather than being perched on the surface. If your intention is to create a deliberately modern, manmade look, do the exact opposite.

Building a waterfall also requires careful arrangement of rocks and stones. In natural waterfalls, the force of the water shapes the rocks as it flows over them and gravity causes smaller stones to tumble down the stream and scatter on the bed. Unless you have a natural watercourse flowing through your garden you'll be relying on a manmade, pumped and recirculated stream. This requires an impervious landscaping fabric or plastic liner to prevent the water from simply seeping away through the earth. As with a garden pond, the plastic layer can eventually be concealed by the surrounding earth, by the rocks themselves, and by marginal planting.

① Appearing as a natural waterfall, this manmade watercourse mimics nature, with large boulders set within the stream and marginal planting introduced for realism.

② A change in the level of the garden can be made less severe by setting large rocks at the base and embedding smaller stones in the bank. Allow plants to grow between the stones to soften the effect.

③ Break up the regularity of a formal flight of garden steps by setting misshapen boulders at the sides.

④ Rounded beach stones can be used in garden landscaping, set within walls, or simply stacked to create an intriguing and quirky display. Stacks of stones like this often appear balanced, but should incorporate a central metal rod to link them.

Continued from page 168.

Structural landscaping of the garden with natural stone is only one method of using this versatile material. Use individual natural stones for their intriguing shapes and textures, and arrange them so that they can be properly appreciated from various angles—in the same way that you would position an obelisk or a statue. A single monolith protruding from the ground like a prehistoric *menhir*, or standing stone, makes a powerful statement. You could even create your own megaliths—a *dolmen* made from four standing stones topped with a large flat stone or a scaled-down version of a stone circle in the fashion of Stonehenge will infuse your garden with an air of myth and mystique. If you'd prefer a more subtle garden design, select round boulders instead of the more rugged varieties to soften a design. Alternatively, imitate the natural occurrence of scree by covering an area with stone chippings.

① A miniature mountainscape is formed by combining rounded and angular boulders with a central bonsai tree, and surrounding them with raked gravel.

② This swimming pool resembles the plunge pool of a waterfall due to the landscaping stonework forming the cascades and rocks softening the edges.

③ Natural stone boulders and scree combine to assimilate these linked, manmade ponds into the surrounding garden.

④ These winding stone sett paths imitate the swirls and eddies of the flowing stream.

⑤ Flat stepping stones and rounded boulders combine with fine gravel, blue slate shards, and beachstones to create a colorful garden pattern.

⑥ Integrate a hot tub and wooden decking into the garden by partially surrounding them with rough stone to create a sunken, natural effect.

Natural landscaping stone is sold in a variety of forms. Large rocks and stones for gardens and for ponds and other water features must be purchased and shipped or delivered by a stoneyard. Garden stones are angular and vary in size, though the most common are approximately 10 inches (25 cm). Stone types include red sandstone, green granite, cream limestone, and black or gray slate. Highly decorative stones in bright candy colors are also available. Some decorative stones are infused with prominent veining. The more rounded boulders, about 8–12 inches (20–30 cm) in size, come in basalt or granite and are typically available in subdued grays and browns or rainbow colors. Large boulders are available in excess of 36 inches (1 m). These are perfect when strong impact is required. When selecting stone for a pond, make sure it is labeled as "fish friendly." Scree, sold in bags, ranges in size from ¾ to 4 inches (2–10 cm). Monoliths, in stone types including limestone, green, blue, black slate, and glistening granite, come in heights from a modest 24 inches (60 cm) to an imposing 60 inches (153 cm) or greater.

① Granite and marble garden rocks
② Boulders within raked sand
③ Multicolored beachstones
④ Boulders incorporated with granite block walls
⑤ Large granite monolith with carved Chinese characters
⑥ Slate slabs and monoliths within raked gravel bed
⑦ Feature stone, riven face
⑧ Beige sandstone boulders, various dimensions
⑨ Random-shaped angular boulders in waterfall
⑩ Limestone boulders
⑪ Gray granite feature stone, incorporated into stone sett paving
⑫ Sandstone rocks around a pond
⑬ Eroded sandstone boulders
⑭ Assorted boulders
⑮ Large limestone pebbles
⑯ Fish-friendly stone

Stone Walls

As far as the style of a wall is concerned, you have the choice between the more formal "dressed" block walls, intended to be laid on mortar, and dry-stone blocks, which are stacked without mortar. Dressed stone blocks are shaped into regular modules for a strong, decorative bond. To produce them, huge blocks are machine-sawn into a range of thicknesses and cut into various lengths and widths. One or more faces are hand-dressed with a split, rough, or a sawn finish, and the blocks are laid with consistently thick mortar joints of about ⅜ inch (1 cm). Face edges may be square or cut with a chamfer to accentuate their shape. Blocks of the same height can be laid much in the same way as brickwork. Different heights can also be incorporated.

Sizes of blocks vary immensely between suppliers, but range from roughly brick shape to lengths of approximately 4–14 inches (10–35 cm) and heights of 3–6 inches (7.5–15 cm). Large blocks may vary between about 20 inches long x 7½ wide x 9.5 high (50 x 19 x 24 cm) to 20 x 9½ x 14 inches (50 x 24 x 35 cm). Long walls should incorporate supporting piers at intervals of 6–10 feet (1.8–3 m). Large structures—particularly boundary walls—are often built from concrete blocks with integral reinforcement. These are usually faced with a thin veneer of natural stone, a cheaper option to building entirely of stone. Slim slabs with a decorative rounded bullnose or shaped edging are available as coping for walls or capping for piers.

①

① Less formal walls can be built by incorporating several sizes of stone blocks—such as this raised terrace and steps—provided you maintain an overall bonding arrangement to ensure the rigidity of the structure.

② The smooth cubes of honed limestone that form the sweeping walls of this pool, contrast with the rough stone cladding of the building.

③ An imposing pier in russet sandstone blocks becomes the centerpiece of a low boundary wall.

④ Befitting a natural setting, this shapely pool is surrounded by walls constructed in random-sized sandstone blocks. Recessed joints create a dry-stone effect.

⑤ Split-faced granite blocks form a dividing wall, with pointed crenelations reminiscent of a medieval castle battlement.

⑥ The intricate structure of this Mediterranean-style wall can be re-created using angular sandstone blocks assembled in a complex, tight-bonding pattern.

Dry-stone walls are constructed without using mortar. The structure is held together by the interlocking assembly of the stones. Methods vary, but all dry-stone walls consist firstly of large, flat foundation stones laid on firm earth. On top of these are laid fairly regular-shaped, flat-edged blocks. Small, irregular-shaped "hearting" stones may be used as infill between the larger blocks. Long, flat "tiestones" are used at intervals to tie the layers together. In one method, the wall becomes narrower as it rises, with wooden "batter frames" setting the angle. At the top, large flat "capstones" are laid, and sometimes a row of vertical coping stones is set atop this. Single-layer dry-stone walls comprise large boulders around which smaller stones are packed.

① Two styles of dry-stone wall are used to create low divisions. One is cut from regular sandstone blocks, the other from laminates of slate.

② In this wall, dry-stacked boulders rely on the interlocking nature of the larger and smaller infill stones.

③ Granite blocks, hand cut into geometric shapes, interlock like a jigsaw puzzle to form a strong, self-supporting structure.

④ Random shapes and sizes of sandstone and granite create this truly rustic wall, with insets for added visual interest.

⑤ Dry-stone walls face the multiple terraces of this garden, where stark brickwork would look out of place.

⑥ Resembling natural rock outcrops— fitting for this woodland setting—thin layers of stone are used here to create dry-stone walls and steps.

Stone block walls are not only strong, reliable, and largely maintenance-free, but also adaptable to different designs. Rough-faced boulders display intriguing shapes and fascinating indents, knobbles, and crevices that produce a wall rich with complex textures. Plain and flat-faced blocks are practical, sturdy, and graceful, with a pleasing linear quality. Colors are as wide-ranging as the materials from which they are hewn. While boundary walls should conform to strict building practices to ensure their safety, walls within the garden can be more flamboyant and decorative—within the boundaries of safety and local regulations of course. A set of steps can be single boulders installed in a bank to provide access from one level to another or sturdy structures comprised of firmly fixed risers of consistent height with flat, level, and firmly bedded treads. Freestanding steps built against a wall can be constructed from coursed, mortared blocks or loose-laid stones (properly interlinked to ensure their integrity).

① Random-coursed granite, mortar jointed
② Random-coursed stone, whitewashed
③ Flat-faced sandstone, dry-wall construction
④ Random-coursed granite, recessed mortar joints
⑤ Floral pattern, dry-stone wall
⑥ Rectangular, random-coursed stonework
⑦ Dry-stone wall with stone fragment insets
⑧ Sandstone blocks, dry-wall construction
⑨ Traditional dry-stone wall with coping
⑩ Thin sandstone slabs, dry-wall construction
⑪ Granite blocks with tile inserts, mortar joints
⑫ Rounded beachstones, mortar pointing
⑬ Dressed sandstone blocks, coursed and jointed
⑭ Rectangular granite blocks, staggered bond
⑮ Dressed sandstone ashlar blocks
⑯ Stacked slate infill

Exterior Architectural Features

Stonework moldings were widely used in classic architectural styles to create or embellish window and door surrounds, keystones above arched openings, lintels, corbels, and quoins, or to add ornate porticos and grand entry steps. Such attention to detail is rarely carried out in modern construction, unless mimicking a classic style. There's no reason why these elegant details can't be added to an otherwise plain property, new or old, provided you're careful not to create an ugly mismatch of styles.

The architecture of days gone by is characterized by popular, fashionable style; and each century boasts its own distinctive hallmarks, though often paying homage to previous incarnations from history. Styles range from plain components, perhaps with chamfered edges to accentuate the shape of blocks, to elaborate scrollwork and detailed carvings of figures or geometric or floral motifs.

While you might still be able to find surviving stonework elements in architectural salvage yards, numerous companies offer replicas in cast stone, which are often created from molds that are based on original profiles. You should not think that these elements are second-best options, however; since they're widely used by professional architects in renovations and new buildings to add a touch of period authenticity. Like solid stonework, the cast variety will weather and assume a pleasing, aged patina, though new items may be affected by efflorescence as salts within the stone migrate to the surface. These salts can be removed quite easily, and eventually disappear.

Installing original architectural features calls for considerable structural remodeling of the house and generally requires the input of professional architects and builders. Cast stonework, which can often be fixed to a surface with an adhesive, presents an alternative. This makes installation on an existing façade a suitable DIY task.

Porches and porticos were popular on houses of the 19th century for aesthetic reasons. They embellished plain façades and provided a measure of protection against the elements. Today, these features can often be assembled from standard architectural elements or custom-made to suit a specific property.

It's also possible to transform the façade of a house, an outbuilding, or a garage by cladding it with stone tiles.

Opposite: Surface-fixed white limestone quoins are attached to the external corners of this rendered wall to match the original stone windows.

Below: A portico constructed from cast limestone complements the period styling on this elegant property.

Exterior Accents

Adding stone accents to an existing façade is easier than you may think. Stone quoins for the external angle of a wall (see page 180) are available in thin panels of cast stone, and they can be installed over existing brickwork. Similarly, corbels and brackets can be easily installed below windowsills, balconies, and parapets. Features designed to be built into the masonry with minimal structural work are also available, though consideration must be given where they bridge a wall to prevent leaks. Porches and porticos can be assembled from columns, architraves, cornices, and entablatures, or custom-made in various styles. Hollow-cast components can save considerable money and time in areas where they do not need to support heavy loads.

Cladding an entire house is typically not a DIY task, and professional installers are required for some products. However, some companies produce easy-to-fix stone tiles that are DIY-friendly. Styles of cladding range from a rough-faced block effect to elegant coursed ashlar blocks or even a veneer of random-shaped slabs. Consider reserving the effect for a bay window, gable wall, chimney, or plain pillar.

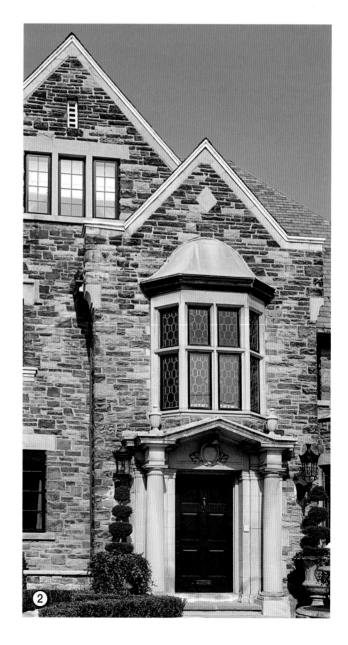

① This house features a distinctive chimney clad in random slate slabs, evoking the style of a cabin from the pioneering West.

② Gothic revival style is typified by stone mullions, imposing porticos, and projecting oriel windows.

③ Stone cladding covers the exterior of this façade, creating a soft blend with the garden path and the overall setting.

④ A modern portico, featuring fluted columns and a roof with toothlike dentils around the molded cornice, enhances the façade of this Georgian mansion.

⑤ Modern cast stonework and reconstituted stone cladding invest a property with an imposing character—at a fraction of the cost of the real thing.

⑥ A simple raised terrace is given a facelift with stone tiles, wall quoins, and cast-limestone balustrades and steps.

Entrances are the first impression visitors receive, and you can use architectural stonework details to create a welcoming effect that reflects your tastes, and the style of the property—perhaps with a hint of what might lie within. The portico, which originated in Ancient Greece, is a type of porch leading to the entrance. A portico consists of side columns that support a flat or apex roof. They can include a plain or elaborate architrave and cornice. A stone door surround consists of side panels or half columns and a lintel, which all lie flat against the wall around the opening. It may be plain or incorporate quoins, elaborately carved figures, floral patterns, or geometric reliefs. Some types even incorporate carved statues at the sides of the door, posed to hold the lintel aloft. Don't just consider the door surround—the door itself is an essential part of the look. A shabby, poorly painted door only detracts from the overall splendor of an opulent portico, elegant porch, or decorative surround.

When planning a stonework porch or surround, take into account its scale in relation to the doorway and the façade of the house: an overlarge structure will seem out of proportion and too dominant, while one that is too small will feel insignificant.

① Half portico, face-fixed, triangular pediment with dentils

② Door surround, fluted columns and lintel, within arched opening

③ Portico with side columns and open pediment roof

④ Door surround with quoins and arched lintel with keystone

⑤ White marble door surround with carved keystone and rosettes

⑥ Rendered stone door surround with arched opening

⑦ Square-carved stone lintel and supporting door jambs

⑧ Cast limestone door surround with half columns, architrave and pediment

⑨ Portico with six fluted columns, Ionic capitals, and flat architrave

⑩ Octagonal portico with four columns, incorporating roof light

⑪ Portico with plain columns and flat entablature, terra-cotta painted

⑫ Four-column portico with flat entablature and balustrading

Window treatments in stonework can consist of a keystone at the top, center of the opening; a complete windowhead with or without an integral keystone; or a windowsill. Some surrounds also incorporate reveals or molded architraves with flat, curved, or triangular profiles. Original items are available from salvage companies, while new replicas in cast stone come in separate easy-to-fix components. "Hood molds" are profiled sections of stonework. These fit over the window opening within a standard brick course.

Walls made of stone or brick might incorporate quoins, the coursed corner blocks (often chamfered to accentuate their shape) at external angles. While fitting original blocks calls for major structural work, cast replicas can simply be installed over an existing surface. Other wall features include corbels and brackets fitted beneath overhanging eaves, sills, parapets, balconies, and ledges. These may be plain-faced or carved with Ionic motifs. Entire walls can be clad with stone tiles, or feature areas clad for contrast with other surfaces.

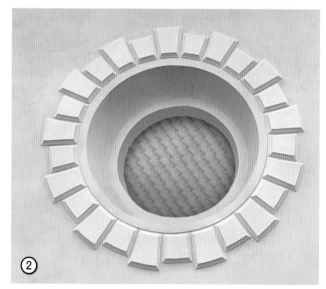

① Gothic arched triple-paned window surround
② Circular window surround with stone quoin effect
③ Sandstone block window frame
④ Riven, coursed stone cladding with decorative window and door details
⑤ Honed marble panels
⑥ Elaborately carved windowhead with corbels
⑦ Limestone block window reveals
⑧ Stone brick cladding on gable siding
⑨ Carved stone door surround, rope effect
⑩ Cast limestone windowsill and windowhead with integral keystone
⑪ Minimal limestone window surround with wall cladding
⑫ Surface-fixed cast limestone quoin panels
⑬ Window framed with quoin effect
⑭ Wall cladding with rectangular blocks and irregular-shaped inset stones
⑮ Stone cladding bricks cut to abut stucco wall

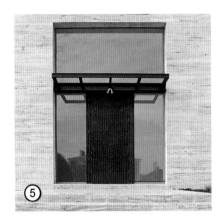

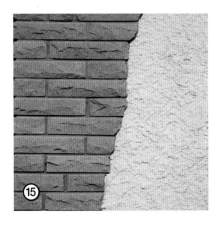

Exterior Decorative Stonework

Ornamental stonework adds emphasis to your yard or garden by adding contrast to the natural, ever-changing surroundings. Statues, obelisks, urns, columns, and sundials draw the eye in a particular direction, while decorative balustrades and screens define spaces. Gazebos and follies provide seating, allowing you to relax and admire the view.

Ornaments in natural stone add a contrast in tone and form to the greenery and floral colors of the garden—the finishing touches that complement the theme you wish to impose, whether that be the classical formality of an 18th-century garden, the rustic simplicity of a traditional country setting, or the sleek modernity of a city yard in an urban townscape.

Statuary forms include characters from Greek mythology, noble Roman emperors, glowering Gothic gargoyles, playful cherubs, and effigies of kings and queens. All these figures lend a sense of history and myth to an outdoor landscape, while abstract sculptures add a modern counterpoint to a natural setting. You will also find animal statues ranging from proud lions and sphinxes to hunting dogs, equine figures to scampering rabbits, and birds from eagles to herons.

Geometric objects, which add a pleasing contrast to the abstract patterns of nature, include needlelike obelisks and pyramids, rounded stone globes on ornate plinths, fluted Corinthian columns with elaborate capitals, and shapely balustrades.

Even the simplicity of a large, carved square block of stone can serve as a decorative focus, especially if it is half concealed by foliage or nestled within a herbaceous border.

The presence of running water is always a source of fascination—both visually and audibly—and a fountain makes a fine decorative touch. If you opt for an elaborate Neapolitan style, you might include multiple shell-like bowls on pedestals, complete with cavorting nymphs and cherubs. Alternatively, you may choose a spouting dolphin, lion, or gargoyle, a graceful Regency-style font, or a modern and graphic globe fountain. You could even add a whimsical touch with a water-spurting frog on a lily pad. Seek out your local suppliers to explore the possibilities.

Not to be forgotten is the ubiquitous garden gnome, to be found in cast stone in many amusing poses. Resist the temptation to paint these jovial characters in their typical gaudy outfits—there's no point in investing in a stone ornament only to conceal it with paint, and their presence will be more intriguing, less brash.

Opposite: These graceful stone urns, decorated with lion heads and floral garlands, are filled with colorful annual plants. They add an elegant touch at the head of a flight of steps.

Below: A simple stone statue, such as this charming female figure perched on a plinth, can be used as a point of interest.

Ornamental Features

The careful positioning of garden ornaments is vital to avoid a jumble of shapes. Stone urns can be used on their own at the corner of a patio or at the end of a path or pergola to give a sense of perspective. Obelisks can also serve the function of defining the end of a path or vista. Use pairs of urns to frame the top of a flight of steps. Ornate finials provide a finishing touch to piers along the length of a wall.

Statues add interest as the centerpiece to a formal garden or to adorn the perimeter of a swimming pool. Smaller figurines of animals can be positioned in the undergrowth of planting beds and shrubberies. Sundials must be positioned in full sun to function without shadows. Birdbaths, while providing an ornate touch, also serve a practical function for feathered friends.

(4)

① Metal gnomons for sundials can be bought separately, which broadens the range of available pedestal styles. This sundial sits on top of a weathered sandstone column.

② The carved stone figure of Summer, holding a bundle of corn, stands at one corner of an enclosure for an elaborate triple Neapolitan fountain. Autumn stands behind clutching her harvest of grapes.

③ Use paving and grass to create an ornamental garden. Circular designs like this one are timeless.

④ Build a waterfall from stones of natural reds, yellows, and grays. Cascading water provides continual decoration.

⑤ Ball finials mounted on the brick piers of this gate transform a plain entrance into an imposing feature.

⑥ A scalloped shell forms the bowl of this wall fountain, sensitively lit to illuminate the garden.

⑤

⑥

Ornamental features for the garden can be divided into water features, such as fountains, birdbaths, pebble pools, cascades, lily pools, and pool surrounds; statuary and urns, including decorative troughs and other planters; partitions, such as balustrades; visual details, such as obelisks, finials, and sundials; and encompassing decorative touches such as lawn edging and wall plaques.

① Georgian baluster-style birdbath
② Small Regency birdbath and pedestal
③ Ground-level lily bowl with scroll feet
④ Ground-level lily bowl or planter
⑤ Stone cascade bowls and pump, variable bowl configuration
⑥ Self-circulating fountain with lion mask
⑦ Three-tiered Eton College replica fountain in cast stone
⑧ Large dolphin fountain
⑨ Tree frog and lily pad fountain
⑩ Triple-ball fountain
⑪ Triple-carp fountain
⑫ Water nymph fountain
⑬ Elephant-head wall fountain
⑭ Pool surround and lion-head wall fountain
⑮ Pool coping, cast limestone
⑯ Sandstone wall fountain waterspout, classical figure

Continued from page 193.

① Sleeping gargoyle
② Greyhound on plinth
③ Saucer-shaped "tazza" cup on fluted neck, with pedestal
④ Bacchus (god of wine) bust on Doric pedestal
⑤ Bust of Pan, cast limestone
⑥ Civitavecchia Equine head replica in cast limestone on plinth
⑦ Andromeda statue, cast limestone
⑧ Planter boxes
⑨ Gallé vase with Art Nouveau leaf design
⑩ Cast limestone gardener figure
⑪ Octagonal jardinière with double-quatrefoil panels
⑫ Bust of Helena, cast white limestone on fluted pedestal
⑬ Jardinière with reticulated rose and rod decoration and rope molding
⑭ Statue of Venus, cast limestone
⑮ Romanesque bowl with coin-molding
⑯ Victorian jardinière with basketwork molding and dragon's feet
⑰ Pebble pot
⑱ Carved lombok plant container
⑲ Lombok stone bowl and stand
⑳ Modern cast limestone sculpture

Continued from page 195.

① Cast-limestone ball and mount on pier
② Round balustrading with square piers, turned balusters, and ball finials
③ Cast-limestone pineapple finial
④ Mushroom bollard, cast limestone
⑤ Smooth cast-limestone pillar bollard with ball top
⑥ Pierced fretwork design screen
⑦ Straight and curved balustrade with chamfered coping
⑧ Sundial for south-facing walls
⑨ Engraved crescent sundial on baluster plinth
⑩ Cast-limestone, Georgian-style sundial
⑪ Engraved Roman sundial face with stainless steel gnomon
⑫ Bishop's finial
⑬ Adam-style finial with drapery swags and lion masks
⑭ Wall plaque depicting a gardener
⑮ Cast-limestone edging in a rope design

Practicalities

Stone is a tough and durable material, but stone floors, countertops, and wall tile do need to be regularly cleaned and maintained if they are to remain in good condition.

DUSTING

Specks of dust and dirt, when ground in by people walking, scratch stone floors and make the surface dull. The most basic way to keep the floor in good condition is to dust it regularly with a good quality rayon dust mop that does not contain oil (oil can soak into the stone and stain it).

DAMP MOPPING

Despite its durability, natural stone is quite sensitive to cleaners that contain acidic elements, such as citrus. When a stone floor becomes dirty, make sure to clean it using a proprietary neutral cleaner with a pH of about 7. Other types of cleaner are likely to leave an unsightly film on the surface of the stone.

Floors can be wet-mopped at least once a week. Rinse with clean water only, as dirty water will leave streaks on the surface.

SURFACE PROTECTION

It's also a good idea to place rugs or mats under planters and items of furniture that might scratch the stone surface. For example, dining chairs, particularly metal ones, should be fitted with rubber feet to prevent scratching when drawn away from the table.

COUNTERTOP CARE

Stone countertops not only need to be kept clean and scratch-free for their looks—cleaning and sealing is essential to protect against germs and bacteria. Water-based cleaner and polish formulas are available specifically for this purpose. Use with microfiber wipes, which penetrate the small irregularities in the stonework and remove dirt without redistributing it, leaving a surface free of chemical residues and odors responsible for causing bacteria. Choose a cleaner that can be used daily, and ensure it is suitable for food-handling surfaces. Some products enrich the natural color of the stone, while providing additional protection against water and other spills.

FLOOR SEALERS

Stone is porous—some types more than others—and polished and honed types are particularly so. A sealer is required to allow the stone to breathe and protect it from spills.

There are two main types of sealers. Topical sealers, or coatings, should be avoided, because they are likely to block the pores of the stone. Silicone-based impregnators are the best option, and these will bar contaminants from entering the stone while allowing any moisture within the stone to evaporate.

Most stone floors should be resealed annually, but how can you be sure that a stone floor needs resealing? A simple method is to place a small amount of water on the surface in a concealed area, then leave it for about 30 seconds before wiping it up. If the water has left a dark patch on the floor, sealing is necessary.

The floor must be thoroughly cleaned before it can be resealed. First, apply the sealer to the surface and leave it for about 15 minutes. If after this time it has completely soaked in, apply

DOORMAT

A good quality doormat placed inside and outside the entranceway will limit dirt, grit, and sand tracked into the home before it scratches the floor. Make sure that you keep the mat clean by frequently shaking it outside to remove debris. Mats should have nonslip backs. Make sure to avoid rubber mats: if they become wet underneath, they are likely to leave a yellow stain on the stone floor.

more. Buff the surface with a buffing pad. Floors that have been neglected may need repolishing, a job best left to the professional, who will use a special powder to restore the sheen.

SHOWER AND BATHROOM CARE
Stone tiles that have been used to clad shower areas may become affected by streaks from bathing products. To deal with these, use a cleaning product specifically designed for cleaning stonework. Disinfect and seal stone bathroom floors using a specialist product that not only cleans but protects against staining. The stone may not be the only area to be affected: the grout joints are particularly susceptible to staining. All-in-one sprays treat both the stone and its grout.

ALGAE, MOSS, AND LICHEN
Paving slabs outdoors can become slippery and unattractive with a build up of moss, lichen, and algae. Sandstone and limestone are particularly prone to being affected by growth. The growth generally appears in areas of low traffic, areas that have no direct sunlight, or areas subject to moisture. Sealers do not prevent the problem; the growth simply appears on top of the sealer. Moss inhibitors alleviate the problem, but the effect will not be lasting— also, avoid moss inhibitors that contain ferrous sulphate, as this may deposit a rust stain on the

paving. You can use a diluted bleach solution to kill growth, so long as you are careful to wash off all traces. Bear in mind that bleach may kill surrounding plant or grass growth. The best way to remove growth is to use a high-pressure water jet. Make sure to avoid acid-based cleaners, which are likely to discolor the stone.

PATIO CLEANERS
Granite, basalt, slate, and quartzite are largely unaffected by acid-based cleaners, but it's still best to avoid these when possible. Sandstone, limestone, marble, and travertine all react badly to acidic products—and limestone can actually be dissolved by hydrochloric acid.

The simplest way to clean outdoor stone paving is to scrub it with soapy water containing an acid-free, soap-based cleaner (make sure to take note of any instructions regarding product suitability for marble or limestone paving). Use a stiff-bristled brush to scrub the soapy water over the stone's surface, then rinse thoroughly using clean water swilled across the surface from a bucket; avoid using a hosepipe, as the pressure from the water jet may dislodge the jointing from between the slabs.

PATIO DE-ICERS
Do not use salt to de-ice patio slabs during freezing conditions, as it is likely to stain the stonework. Instead, use regular sand.

WEED GROWTH
Paved outdoor surfaces can become afflicted with weeds growing between the slabs. The easiest way to prevent them from growing is to brush the surface regularly, which prevents them from growing enough to spread. If this fails, weedkiller can be applied, but ensure it is specially formulated for paving, which is less likely to stain the paving or kill adjacent plants or lawn.

Glossary

Architrave: A main beam resting atop columns; the molded frame around a window or doorway.

Ashlar: Masonry made of large, square-cut stones used to face stone walls.

Backsplash: A vertical, impervious surface behind a countertop or vanity unit.

Baluster: A short pillar or column used in series to support a rail.

Balustrade: A railing supported by balusters.

Basalt: Dark, fine-grained volcanic rock.

Batter frame: A wooden frame used as a guide to the angle of a drystone wall, sometimes used in conjunction with stringlines.

Bush-hammered: A finish for stone whereby it is pounded to produce pits and grooves.

Capital: The crowning component of a column or pilaster.

Cast stone: Stone-based material cast in molds to produce stonework items.

Cladding: Stone slabs, blocks, or tiles used to cover a building façade.

Cobblestone (or cobble): A small round stone formerly used to surface roads.

Coping: A row of stones (or another weathered material) used to finish the top of a wall.

Corbel: A component jutting out from a wall, which supports a structure above it.

Corinthian: Classical order of architecture denoted by columns with flared capitals (often adorned with acanthus leaves).

Countertop: A horizontal surface in the kitchen used for food preparation.

Dolmen: A megalithic burial chamber.

Doric: Classical order of architecture denoted by a plain, sturdy column resting on rounded molding.

Dressed: Stonework that has been shaped and finished.

Dry-stacked stone: A stone wall built without mortar joints.

Filled: A finish for stonework, such as travertine, in which the tiny voids in the surface are filled with epoxy resin.

Finial: A distinctive ornament at the apex of a roof, pier, or other structure.

Flamed: A stonework finish where the surface is heated to burst the crystals within and give a nonslip, aged look.

Folly: An ornamental building that has no practical purpose.

Frieze: The panel beneath a fireplace mantel and sides, often decorated.

Gabion: A wirework or (historically) wickerwork container filled with rock and used in the construction of retaining walls.

Gazebo: A roofed structure that gives an open view of the surrounding area.

Going: The horizontal distance between the face of the first and last risers in a staircase.

Granite: Extremely hard igneous rock with a crystalline structure and a broad color range.

Gravel: A loose aggregation of water-worn or pounded stones.

Grout: The material used to seal the gaps between tiles or slabs.

Hearting stones: Small, irregularly shaped stones used as infill in a dry-stone wall.

Honed: A textured dull finish for stone, which is also nonslip.

Hood mold: A profiled stonework component fitted over a window opening in a standard brick course.

Igneous: Rock that has solidified from lava or magma.

Impregnator: A sealer that penetrates the pores of stonework.

Jerusalem stone: The generic term for meleke, a type of dolomitic limestone quarried in the Jerusalem area of Israel.

Keystone: The central stone at the summit of an arch, which locks the structure together.

Limestone: Hard sedimentary rock of calcium carbonate or dolomite.

Marble: A hard metamorphic form of limestone, typically white with mottling and veining.

Megalith: A large stone that forms a prehistoric monument.

Menhir: A megalithic standing stone.

Mosaic: A picture or pattern created by arranging small colored pieces of stone.

Obelisk: Stone pillar with a square or rectangular cross-section and pyramidal top, used as a monument or landmark.

Pergola: A framework of uprights and rafters covered with climbing plants.

Pillow finish: A wrinkled, irregular finish for the edges of stone tiles and slabs.

Porphyry: A hard, fine-grained igneous rock containing crystals of feldspar.

Portico: A roofed structure on columns attached to a building, typically at the front entrance.

Quartzite: Compact, hard, granular metamorphic rock, predominantly quartz.

Quoin: A stone used to form the external angle of a wall.

Reconstituted stone: Stone aggregate used in conjunction with resins and cast in molds to produce stonework items.

Rise: The vertical distance between the treads of a staircase.

Riser: The vertical part of a step, on which the tread rests.

Riven: The undulating face of stone that has been split.

Run: The horizontal distance between the treads in a staircase.

Sandstone: Sedimentary rock of sand or quartz grains.

Sanitaryware: Fittings in the bathroom, such as the toilet, basin, and bidet.

Scree (and screescape): A mass of small, loose stones that cover a slope, which can be used in a garden as ground cover.

Sedimentary: Stone formed from sediment deposited by water or air.

Sett: A small sawn or split-faced cube of stone used in paving.

Slab: A lengthwise cut of a solid block of quarried stone.

Slate: Fine-grained gray, green, or blue metamorphic rock that can be split into smooth, flat pieces.

Soapstone: A soft rock consisting mainly of the mineral talc.

String (or stringboard): The side component of a staircase, into which the treads and risers are inserted.

Tesserae: The individual pieces of a mosaic.

Throughs (or tiestones): Long, flat stones used at intervals to tie together the leaves of a drystone wall.

Topical sealer: A sealer which forms a coating on top of stonework.

Travertine: White or light-colored calcareous rock deposited from mineral springs.

Tread: The horizontal part of a step, on which you walk.

Tumbled: A rustic smooth, polished finish created by tumbling the stone in a drum with a silicon carbide abrasive.

Uncalibrated: Tiles or slabs in a batch, which have varying thicknesses.

Vanity unit: A bathroom fitting incorporating a basin.

Yorkstone: A hardwearing variety of sandstone originating in the north of England.

Resource Guide

The following list of manufacturers, associations, and outlets is meant to be a general guide to additional industry and product-related sources. It is not intended as a complete listing of products and manufacturers represented in this book. All of the garden landscapers listed here work with stone and all have photographs of their work included.

ASSOCIATIONS

Masonry Veneer Manufacturers Association
1156 15th Street NW, Suite 900
Washington, D.C. 20005, U.S.A.
Tel: 202 785 3232
www.masonryveneer.org

Marble Institute of America
28901 Clemens Rd, Ste 100
Cleveland, OH 44145, U.S.A.
Tel: 440 250 9222

CAST RECONSTITUTED STONE

Chilstone Ltd
garden ornaments and structures, architectural cast stone
Fordcombe Road
Langton Green, Kent TN3 0RE, U.K.
Tel: +44 (0)1892 740866

Haddonstone (U.S.A.) Ltd
garden ornaments and structures, architectural cast stone, fireplaces
201 Heller Place
Bellmawr, NJ 08031, U.S.A.
Tel: 856 931 7011
www.haddonstone.com

Haddonstone (U.K.) Ltd
The Forge House
East Haddon
Northampton NN6 8DB, U.K.
Tel: +44 (0)1604 770711
www.haddonstone.com

GENERAL

Amlink Marble
2252 Ellsworth Road
Ypsilanti, MI 48197, U.S.A.
Tel: 734 528 9099
www.amlinkmarble.com

BC Designs
The Design Works
Allens Farm, Tye Road
Elmstead Market
Essex C07 7BN, U.K.
Tel: +44 (0)1206 827100
www.bcdesign.co.uk

English Fireplaces
Unit 6, The Brows
Farnham Road, Liss
Hampshire GU33 6JG, U.K.
Tel: +44 (0)1730 897600
www.englishfireplaces.co.uk

Fire Stone
outdoor rooms
12400 Portland Ave South, Ste 195
Burnsville, MN 55337
Tel: 866 303 4028
www.firestonehp.com

Rock Unique
Sundridge, Sevenoaks
Kent TN14 6ED, U.K.
Tel: +44 (0)1959 565608
www.rock-unique.com

GENERAL STONEWORK

U.S.A. Stone
kitchens, bathrooms, fireplaces, carvings, balustrades, exterior
1785 N. Lapeer Road
Oxford, MI 48371, U.S.A
(also Nashville, TN; Columbia, SC)
Tel: 248 628 8915

STONE CARE

Brightstone, Inc.
stone cleaners, sealers, restorers
1636 240th Street
Harbor City, CA 90710, U.S.A.
Tel: 800 899 7193

Stone Care International Inc.
stone cleaners, polishes, grout care
P.O. Box 703
Owings Mills, MD 21117, U.S.A.
Tel: 800 839 1654
www.stonecare.com

STONE CLADDING

Cultured Stone
stone veneer, interior and exterior
Owens Corning Masonry Products LLC
1 Owens Corning Parkway
Toledo, OH 43659, U.S.A.
Tel: 800 255 1727
www.culturedstone.com

Stone Master U.S.A.
stone veneer
246 North 6th Avenue
Manville, NJ 08835, U.S.A.
Tel: 909 203 9448
www.stonemasterusa.com

STONE COUNTERTOPS

All Granite & Marble Corp.
natural stone
1A Mt. Vernon Street
Ridgefield Park, NJ 07660, U.S.A.
Tel: 201 440 6855
www.marble.com

CaesarStone U.S.A.
engineered quartz stone
6840 Hayvenhurst Ave, Suite 100
Van Nuys, CA 91406, U.S.A.
Tel: 818 779 0999

Rock Tops
Matts Hill Farm, Matts Hill Lane
Sittingbourne ME9 7UY, U.K.
Tel: +44 (0)1634 264 606
www.rock-tops.co.uk

STONE FIREPLACES & STAIRCASES

Boden & Ward
Ox-House Farm, Brington Road
Flore, Northampton NN7 4NQ, U.K.
Tel: +44 (0)1327 349081

Ian Knapper
Mobberley Garage
Tean Road, Cheadle
Staffordshire ST10 1TZ, U.K.
Tel: +44 (0)1538 722733
www.ianknapper.com

STONE FLOORS

Indigenous Ltd
Cheltenham Road, Burford
Oxfordshire OX18 4JA, U.K.
Tel: +44 (0)1993 824200
www.indigenoustiles.com

STONE ORNAMENTS & FURNISHINGS

Stone Living
accessories, statues, furnishings
U.K.
Tel: +44 (0)1530 515268
www.stoneliving.com

Stone World Inc.
accessories, statues, furnishings
1699 Peachtree Parkway
Cumming, GA 30041, U.S.A.
Tel: 770 888 0550
www.stoneworldinc.com

STONE TILES & SLABS

Jerusalem Stone
319 West 79th Terrace
Kansas City, MO 64114, U.S.A.
Tel: 816 444 4405
www.jerusalemstoneusa.com

Jerusalem Stone NY LLC
1072 Atlantic Avenue
Brooklyn, NY 11238, U.S.A.
Tel: 718 783 2527
www.jerusalemstoneny.com

Mandarin Stone Ltd
stone tiles, sanitaryware
Head Office, Unit 1
Wonastow Industrial Estate
Monmouthshire NP25 5JB
Wales, U.K.
Tel: +44 (0)1600 715444
www.mandarinstone.com

Original Style Ltd
stone tiles, sanitaryware
Falcon Road
Sowton Industrial Estate
Exeter EX2 7LF, U.K.
Tel: +44 (0)1392 473000

Rock Unique
stone flooring, stone ornaments
Dryhill Lane, Sundridge
Sevenoaks, Kent TN14 6ED, U.K.
Tel: +44 (0)1959 565608
www.rock-unique.com

Stone Age Ltd
stone flooring, countertops,
sanitaryware, fire surrounds,
staircases
Unit 3, Parsons Green Depot
Parsons Green Lane
London SW6 4HH, U.K.
Tel: +44 (0)20 7384 9090
www.estone.co.uk

Stone Design Inc.
stone flooring, tiling
551 Mitchell Road
Glendale Heights, IL 60139, U.S.A.
Tel: 800 424 1332
(also Indiana; Wisconsin)
www.stone-design.com

Stone Tile International Inc.
stone tiles
1451 Castlefield Avenue
Toronto M6M 1Y3
Canada
Tel: 416 515 9000
www.stone-tile.com

Tiles & Stones Inc
stone tiles, slabs, countertops
1777 NW 72 Avenue
Miami, FL 33126, U.S.A.
Tel: 305 718 8133
www.tilesandstones.com

DECORATED STONE TILES

Stone Impressions
8495 Redwood Creek Lane
San Diego, CA 92126, U.S.A.
Tel: 858 274 3400
www.stoneimpressions.com

LANDSCAPE ARCHITECTS

Clemens and Associates, Inc.
1290 Lejano Lane
Sante Fe, NM 87501, U.S.A
Tel: 505 982 4005
www.clemensandassociates.com

The Cushman Design Group, Inc.
100 Mountain Road, P.O. Box 655
Stowe, VT 05672, U.S.A
Tel: 802 253 2169
Fax. 802 253 2160
www.cushmandesign.com

Hannabelle Garden Co.
Cambridge, VT, U.S.A
Tel: 802 644 8749

Insight Design
1141 Clay Point Rd
Colchester, VT 05446, U.S.A
Tel: 802 893 2446

St Griswold Co, Inc.
35 Industrial Ave
Williston, VT 05495, U.S.A
Tel: 802 658 0201
www.stgriswold.com

Lang Farm Nursery
51 Upper Main St
Essex Jct, VT 05452, U.S.A.
Tel: 802 878 5720

Wagner McCann Studio
7 Marble Ave
Burlington, VT 05401, U.S.A.
Tel: 802 864-0010

Andrea Morgante
56 Mechanicsville Rd
Hinesburg, VT 05461, U.S.A.
Tel: 802 482 5120

Index

Acknowledgments

The publishers would like to thank the following companies for their invaluable assistance: Amorim, Anderson Floors, Armstrong, Artwork in Architectural Glass Studios, Award Hardwood Floors, Bettini Tile Service, Carina Works, Congoleum, Daltile, Duro Design, Dynamic Stone, Florida Tile, Forbo, GuildCraft Carpets, Indigenous, Interior Leather Surfaces, Kährs, Lauzon, Mandarin Stone, Mannington, Merida Meridian, Mullican Flooring, Nourison, Pergo, Quick-Step, The Rug Company, Seattle Glass Block and Teragren.

2 C.P. Hart

4–5 Ian Fleming/Redcover.com

6 Fotolia.com

7 iStockphoto.com

8–9 1 Ashley Morrison/Redcover.com; 2 Mandarin Stone;

3 Colin Sharp/Habitat/Redcover.com; 4 Winfried Heinze/Redcover.com, Designer: Grant White; 5 Rock Unique

10–11 1 Carolyn L. Bates Photography/Designer: REM Development; 2, 3 Andreas von Einsiedel Archive/Designers: John Pawson (2), Anna & Aib Barwick (3); 4 Jean Maurice/Redcover.com, Designer: Anne Bedel; 6 Haddonstone; 7 Indigenous

12–13 1 Carolyn L. Bates Photography/Architect: Brad Rabinowitz; 2 Andreas von Einsiedel Archive/Designer: Dorthe Wehmeyer; 3 Mandarin Stone; 4, 5 Indigenous

14–15 1 iStockphoto.com; 2–4 Porcelanosa; 5 Rohl

16–17 1 Andreas von Einsiedel/Designer: Candy & Candy; 2 Andrew Twort/Redcover.com; 3 Mandarin Stone; 4 Carolyn L. Bates Photography/Architect: Nils Luderowski; 5 Andreas von Einsiedel Archive/Designer: Hans-Otto Beute

18–19 1, 5, 7 Rock Unique/Contractors: Generating Gardens (1), Creating Landscapes (7); 2 Fotolia.com; 3, 4, 6 Carolyn L. Bates Photography/Designers: The Cushman Design Group (3), Jon Lang (4), Hannabelle Garden Company (6)

20–21 1 DLILLC/Corbis; 2 Fotolia.com; 3 Michael Freeman/Redcover.com; 4 iStockphoto.com

22–23 1 Simon McBride/redcover.com; 2, 3 Fire Stone; 4 Hickory Dickory Decks/Drew Cunnigham, Canada; 5 Rock Unique

24–25 1, 2, 4 iStockphoto.com; 3, 6 Rock Unique/Contractor: The Outdoor Room (6); 5 Stone Living

26–27 1 Carolyn L. Bates Photography/Designer: Wagner McCann Studio; 2 Hickory Dickory Decks/Drew Cunnigham, Canada; 3 Fotolia.com; 4 Scott Van Dyke/Corbis

28 Quickimage/Emilio Rodriguez/Redcover.com

29 Porcelanosa

30–31 1, 6 Andreas von Einsiedel Archive/Designers: Dorthe Wehmeyer (1), Athena Strutt (6); 2 Laufen; 3 C.P. Hart; 4 Ashley Morrison/Redcover.com; 5 Evan Sklar/Redcover.com; 7 Roca

32–33 1–12, 16–20 Fotolia.com;13 iStockphoto.com, 14 Laufen

34–35 1 iStockphoto.com; 2 Carolyn L. Bates Photography/Architect: Moran & Associates; 3 Ed Reeve/Redcover.com, Designer: Work Ltd; **4** Warren Smith/Redcover.com

36–37 1 Andrew Woods/Redcover.com; 2 Mandarin Stone; 3 Pergo;

4 iStockphoto.com

40–41 Daltile

42–43 1, 3, 4 Porcelanosa; 2 Andreas von Einsiedel Archive/Designer: Candy & Candy; 5 Carolyn L. Bates Photography/Architect: Looney Ricks Kiss Architects

44–45 1, 2 Indigenous; 3 Porcelanosa; 4 Villeroy and Boch

46–47 Daltile

48–49 1 Abacus Direct; 2 Fotolia.com; 3, 4 Porcelanosa; 5 Ed Reeve/Redcover.com, Designer: Monica Mauti Equihua; 6 Laufen

50–51 1 Carolyn L. Bates Photography/Designer: REM Development; 2 Daltile; 3 Laufen; 4 Porcelanosa

52–53 1–10 Daltile; 11–12 Corbis

54–55 1–6 Corbis; 7 Daltile; 8–12 Amlink

56–57 1 Bathrooms International; 2 Carolyn L. Bates Photography/Designer: Sheridan Interiors; 3, 5 Porcelanosa; 4 Roca

58–59 1–3 Indigenous; 4 Laufen; 5 Porcelanosa

60–61 1–11 Daltile; 12 Indigenous

62–63 1–5 Indigenous; 6–8 Corbis; 9–12 Amlink

64–65 1 Winfried Heinze/Redcover.com; 2 Carolyn L. Bates Photography/Architects: Sellers and Co; 3 Andreas von Einsiedel Archive/Designer: Elisabeth Brooks; 4 Porcelanosa

66–67 1 Duravit; 2, 3 Porcelanosa; 4 Roca

68–69 1 Duravit; 2 Abacus Direct; 3 Ken Hayden/Redcover.com, Designer: Jonathan Reed; 4 Stone Living; 5 Porcelanosa

70–71 1–5 Indigenous; 6 Porcelanosa

72–73 1–10 Amlink; 11–16 Daltile

74–75 Daltile

76–77 1 Porcelanosa; 2 Grey Crawford/Redcover.com; 3 Johnny Bouchier/Redcover.com; 4 Grant Govier/Redcover.com

78–79 1 Daltile; 2 Porcelanosa; 3 Graham Atkins-Hughes/Redcover.com; 4 Carolyn L. Bates Photography/Designer: The Cushman Design Group

80–81 Amlink

82–83 1–6, 8–16 Amlink; 7 Corbis

84–85 1, 2 Andreas von Einsiedel Archive/Designers: Manhattan Loft Company (1), Anna & Aib Barwick (2); 3 Ian Fleming/Redcover.com; 4 Jake Fitzjones/Redcover.com; 5 Warren Smith/Redcover.com

86–87 1 Ed Reeve/Redcover.com; 2 Carolyn L. Bates Photography/Designer: The Cushman Design Group; 3 Duravit; 4–6 Indigenous

88–89 1, 11–16 Amlink; 2–10 Bettini Tile Service

90–91 1, 6–8, 12, 13, 15, 16 Bettini Tile Service; 2, 3, 11, 14 Amlink; 4, 5 Corbis; 9, 10 Daltile

92–93 1 Kohler; 2, 6 Hakatai; 3 Chris Drake/Redcover.com; 4 Porcelanosa; 5 Laufen

94–95 1 Laufen; 2–4 Daltile; 5, 6 Fotolia.com; 7 Grant Govier/Redcover.com

96–99 Daltile

106 Fernando Bengoechea/Corbis

107 Abode/Beateworks/Corbis

108–109 1, 3, 4 Fotolia.com; 2 Paul Ryan/Redcover.com; 5 Andrew Woods/Redcover.com; 6 iStockphoto.com; 7 Haddonstone

110–111 1 Indigenous; 2 Ken Hayden/Redcover.com; 3 Duravit; 4 Stone Living; 5 Carolyn L. Bates Photography/Architect: Sellers and Co; 6 Fabio Lombrici/Redcover.com; Designer: Juan Carlos Sanchez;

112–113 1, 2, 5–8 Fotolia.com; 3 Ken Hayden/Redcover.com, Designer: Jonathan Reed; 4 Michael Robinson/Beateworks/Corbis; 9, 12 Peter Anderson/Steven Wooster; 10, 11 Haddonstone

114–115 1, 5 Chilstone; 2–4, 6–8 Stone Living

116 Ian Knapper

117 Rock Unique

118–119 1, 3, 6 Stone Age/The John Hytch Photography Partnership; 2 Porcelanosa; 4 Haddonstone; 5 Rock Tops/Thoroughly Wood

120–121 1 Perrin and Rowe; 2 Rohl; 3, 4, 6, 7 Rock Tops/Thoroughly Wood; 5 Stone Age/The John Hytch Photography Partnership

122–123 1 Perrin and Rowe; 2, 3 Fotolia.com; 4 Bathrooms International; 5 Roca; 6, 7 Rohl; 8–10, 12 Rock Tops/Thoroughly Wood; 11 Rock Unique; 13–20 Stone Age/The John Hytch Photography Partnership

124–125 1, 4 Porcelanosa; 2 C.P. Hart; 3 Rohl; 5, 6 Stone Age/The John Hytch Photography Partnership

126–127 1, 2 BC Designs; 3–7 Fotolia.com; 8, 9 C.P. Hart; 10 Bathrooms International; 11 Porcelanosa; 12–15 Stone Age/The John Hytch Photography Partnership; 16 Stone Living

128–129 1 Andreas von Einsiedel Archive/Designer: Ulla Huebener; 2 Carolyn L. Bates Photography/Architect: Sandra Vitzthum; 3, 4 Fotolia.com; 5 Ian Knapper; 6 Khars

130–131 1, 2 Boden and Ward; 3–13 English Fireplaces; 14 Fotolia.com; 15, 16 Haddonstone; 17–20 Ian Knapper

132–133 1 Boden and Ward; 2 Stone Age/The John Hytch Photography Partnership; 3 Andreas von Einsiedel Archive/Designer: Nona von Haefen; 4 Fotolia.com; 5 iStockphoto.com

134–135 1 Boden & Ward; 2–4, 6–9 Fotolia.com; 5 iStockphoto.com; 10 Rock Unique; 11, 12 Stone Age/John Hytch Photography

136 Carolyn L. Bates Photography/Contractor: GC Wright Construction

137 Rausch Classics

138–139 1, 5 Carolyn L. Bates Photography/Designers: The Cushman Design Group (1), Wagner McCann Studio (5); 2 Fire Stone; 3 APSP; 4 iStockphoto.com

140–141 1, 2 APSP; 3, 4 Carolyn L. Bates Photography/Designers: Insight Design (3), Wagner McCann Studio (4); 5, 6 Rock Unique

142–143 1 APSP; 2 Carolyn L. Bates Photography/Designer: Insight Design; 3–8 Fotolia.com; 9–12 Rock Unique

144–145 1, 6 Rausch Classics; 2, 3 Rock Unique/Contractor: Generating Gardens (3); 4, 5 iStockphoto.com

146–147 1–3, 5–12 Rock Unique/Contractors: Basewood Design (1), Creative Landscapes (3), Langdale Landscapes (9), The Outdoor Room (11, 12); 4 Daltile

148–149 1, 3, 5 Fotolia.com; 2 Carolyn L. Bates Photography/Designer: The Cushman Design Group; 4 iStockphoto.com; 6 Rock Unique; 7 Rausch Classics

150–151 1 APSP; 2–10 Fotolia.com; 11 Roch Unique

152–153 1 APSP; 2 iStockphoto.com; 3–5 Rock Unique/Contractor: Creative Landscapes (3); 6 Fire Stone

154–155 1 Fotolia.com; 2–12 Rock Unique

156–157 1 Fotolia.com; 2, 3, 5 Rock Unique/Contractor: Creative Landscapes (5); 4 iStockphoto.com; 6 Hickory Dickory Decks/Drew Cunnigham, Canada

158–159 1–7 Fotolia.com; 8–12 Rock Unique

166 Carolyn L. Bates Photography/Designer: Insight Design

167 Fotolia.com

168–169 1 APSP; 2–4 iStockphoto.com

170–171 1 Fotolia.com; 2, 3 APSP; 4 Greg Ryan/Sally Beyer/Redcover.com; 5 Ron Evans/Redcover.com; 6 Rodney Hyett; Elizabeth Whiting Asc/Corbis

172–173 1–3, 5–9, 14–16 Fotolia.com; 4 iStockphoto.com; 10 Hickory Dickory Decks/Drew Cunnigham, Canada; 11 Carolyn L. Bates Photography/Designer: St Griswold Company; 12, 13 APSP

174–175 1 Carolyn L. Bates Photography/Designer: Clemens and Associates; 2, 4 APSP; 3 Rausch Classics; 5 Fotolia.com; 6 Andreas von Einsiedel Archive/Designers: Holger Stewen

176–177 1, 4, 6 Carolyn L. Bates Photography/Designers: Wagner McCann Studio (1), Andrea Morgante (4), The Cushman Design Group (6); 2 Andreas von Einsiedel Archive/Designer: Dorthe Wehmeyer; 3 Fotolia.com; 5 APSP

178–179 1 Fortress Iron; 2–14 Fotolia.com; 15 Rock Unique; 16 Divine Construction

180 Rock Unique

181 Haddonstone

182–183 1, 3 Hickory Dickory Decks/Drew Cunnigham, Canada; 2 Fotolia.com; 4 Chilstone; 5 iStockphoto.com; 6 Haddonstone

184–185 1 Chilstone; 2–6 Fotolia.com; 7 iStockphoto.com; 8–12 Haddonstone

186–187 1 Chilstone; 2–9, 15 Fotolia.com; 10, 12 Haddonstone; 11, 13 iStockphoto.com; 14 Fortress Iron

188 Greg Ryan/Sally Beyer/Redcover.com

189 iStockphoto.com

190–191 1 iStockphoto.com; 2, 5, 6 Haddonstone; 3 Eric Crichton/Corbis; 4 Elliott Kaufman/Beateworks/Corbis

192–193 1, 2, 5–12, 14, 15 Haddonstone; 3, 4, 13 Stone Living; 16 Rock Unique

194–195 1–3 Chilstone; 4–16 Haddonstone; 17–20 Stone Living

196–197 1–4, 6 Chilstone; 5, 7–15 Haddonstone